"Here is some of the richest f
years spent studying and constructing liturgical language. If not for the vast historical and theological information Ramshaw offers, this book would be valuable just for her questions: Can yards of red cloth speak Holy Spirit? Are individual chairs for worship best for families? Is 'ordinary' the best word for the green season? This book makes me want to know my Christian ancestors."

> —The Rev. Melinda A. Quivik, PhD
> Editor-in-Chief, *Liturgy*
> President, North American Academy of Liturgy

"Here is a book to make us think—with Gail Ramshaw, in the company of saints, and for ourselves—about what 'Sunday' could be if we took to heart the wisdom from the past assembled in these pages. As sagacious as ever, and in the most personal voice in her own writing since *Under the Tree of Life* twenty years ago, Gail Ramshaw continues to offer us vivid, winsome, lively reading. A wonderful book."

> —Stephen Burns
> Professor of Liturgical and Practical Theology
> Pilgrim Theological College
> University of Divinity, Melbourne, Australia

"Gail Ramshaw delights and challenges as she probes the lives and writings of saints through the centuries, inviting her readers to think deeply about what Christians say and do in Sunday worship. With more questions than answers, she encourages her readers to re-imagine and re-invigorate their worship practices."

> —Ruth Meyers
> Dean of Academic Affairs and Hodges-Haynes
> Professor of Liturgics
> Church Divinity School of the Pacific

"Gail Ramshaw enjoys conversations. The gathering around the table with her and other guests generates conversation with fascinating stopping points and vistas, which always return to a center point of a love for the church and liturgy. This book offers a series of conversations with friends of Gail Ramshaw. These 'twenty-four elders' (Rev. 4:4), invited from the list of the church's long history, each provide the starting point for a spirited interchange on the liturgical traditions and faith convictions their lives embody. An ancient friend like Justin Martyr speaks of Sunday while a modern one like Dorothy Day muses on prayers of intercession for those homeless and in need. Anecdotes and observations about contemporary liturgical concerns limn a portrait of the liturgy of life. This series of conversations will provide hours of thought, prayer, and occasional smiles for those who pull up a chair at the table and join in."

—Rev. Michael G. Witczak, SLD
Associate Professor of Liturgical Studies and
Sacramental Theology
The Catholic University of America

Saints on Sunday

*Voices from our past
enlivening our worship*

Gail Ramshaw

LITURGICAL PRESS
Collegeville, Minnesota

www.litpress.org

Cover design by Monica Bokinskie.

Cover art: Wassily Kandinski, *All Saints Day I*, 1911.

Scripture quotations are from New Revised Standard Version Bible © 1989 National Council of the Churches of Christ in the United States of America. Used by permission. All rights reserved worldwide.

"By All Your Saints" © 2006 Augsburg Fortress, Minneapolis, MN. All rights reserved. Used by permission.

"Canticle of Brother Sun" © 1973 Franciscan Media, Cincinnati, OH. All rights reserved. Permission granted by Franciscan Media.

"Great God, Your Love Has Called Us Here." Words: Brian Wren. © 1975, rev. 1995 Hope Publishing Company, Carol Stream, IL 60188. All rights reserved. Used by permission.

"There in God's Garden" © 1975 Hinshaw Music, Inc., Chapel Hill, NC. All rights reserved. Used by permission.

1   2   3   4   5   6   7   8   9

Library of Congress Cataloging-in-Publication Data

Names: Ramshaw, Gail, 1947– author.
Title: Saints on Sunday / Gail Ramshaw.
Description: Collegeville, Minnesota : Liturgical Press, 2018. | Includes
    bibliographical references.
Identifiers: LCCN 2017059285 (print) | LCCN 2018028086 (ebook) |
    ISBN 9780814645833 (ebook) | ISBN 9780814645581
Subjects: LCSH: Christian saints—Meditations. | Church year
    meditations. | Devotional calendars—Catholic Church. |
    Worship—Miscellanea.
Classification: LCC BV65 (ebook) | LCC BV65 .R36 2018 (print) | DDC
    270.092/2—dc23
LC record available at https://lccn.loc.gov/2017059285

Contents

Preface

In the book of Revelation, twenty-four white-robed elders are seated around the throne of the Lamb, and at Sunday worship, we join with them in singing praises to God. The essays in this book look to another twenty-four of the church's faithful departed, whose ministry was extraordinary while they were alive, in hopes that even now when they are dead, their words might illumine our worship and assist our efforts at liturgical renewal.

Some of these twenty-four elders are universally revered as saints and honored as models of the liturgical life. Others of these twenty-four, although less famous, surprise us with their insight and offer useful suggestions, or at least pose bothersome questions, as we enact worship. I intend by my title, *Saints on Sunday*, to address my essays both to those Christians who formally canonize their dead and to those who name all the baptized, alive and dead, as saints of God. It is about Sunday worship that I am most concerned, for it is primarily on Sunday that Christians, as the communion of saints, gather to hear the Word and share the meal.

Throughout these essays, whether discussing the triune God, the *ordo* of the liturgy, or various attendant issues, I have asked whether the wisdom of these beloved dead might improve and deepen and widen and enrich our communal worship. In some essays, I can identify and applaud specific directions pointed out by these believers. In others, I throw up my hands, both in bewilderment and in invocation, admitting that even though I have heard the voices from the past, acceptable solutions may be quite beyond me. (After one of his lectures, Marcus Borg was asked, "But how do you know that you're right?" And he responded, "I don't know. I don't know that I'm right.")[1] Perhaps, indeed, my questions are more useful to you than are my answers.

Thank you for joining me in liturgical conversation.

Chapter

Assembling on Sunday with Justin

B orn in about 100, Justin was a seeker after truth, who in about 135, after considering various schools of philosophical thought and their moral teachings, found the truth in Jesus Christ and became the first great Christian apologist, a believer seeking to explain Christian faith and practice to the outsider. An uncircumcised Gentile originally from Samaria, he established his own Christian catechetical school in Rome. Hoping to convince Jews of the truth of Christ, he crafted a lengthy exegetical discussion of the relationship between the Hebrew scriptures and Jesus. Justin is "the first early Christian writer to make extended use of the name 'Christian' and does it with pride and confidence,"[1] and this during a time when such open confession of the faith could lead to execution. Indeed, while Marcus Aurelius was Roman emperor, probably in 165, Justin and six companions in the faith were condemned to death and beheaded on June 1. Because of his eminence in the tradition, subsequent centuries of Christians have honored him with the name Justin Martyr. May we join him in confessing with pride and confidence that we are Christians, whatever befalls.

Writing to the Roman emperor Antoninus Pius a description of Christian belief and practice, Justin composed what is our earliest complete narrative of the order for Christian worship. This First Apology of Justin has had incalculable significance, if not to the Roman emperor, then to current students of liturgy. (Do you know this passage by heart?) Justin outlined a simple order as the standard in his community; the meeting takes place on Sunday; the ritual has "a presider"; the reader is not the same person as the presider; the event includes readings from both the Hebrew scriptures and the Gospels; the weekly event is titled "eucharist" and the great prayer over the bread and wine "a thanksgiving"; he mentions a kiss of peace and communal intercessions; he describes a subsequent visitation to absent members; he connects this meeting with Christian care for the needy. One can see this description of the worship that he attended in Rome as the agenda for contemporary liturgical reformers.

For it is often the case that historical investigation conducted by liturgists is prompted by the desire to find, not merely a record of past practice, but a substantiation for future reforms. Granting that much religious ritual is an essentially conservative phenomenon—we danced last year at the full moon, and the rains came, so let's dance again this year—many liturgists search for an ideal moment in the past (ah, and when was that?) that might inspire the inadequate or wrongheaded present to move toward a revivified future. Admittedly, in the twenty-first century, this Christian digging through murky yesterdays toward radiant tomorrows has become especially complicated, thanks both to our dear liturgical historians demonstrating that, alas, we cannot actually know the past and to the postmodern conviction that each age can enjoy no more than its own version of truth. Yet the habit continues, and thus when Christians are accused of instigating innovations in worship, they often try to take refuge in the claim that they are merely resurrecting a past that, like poor Thomas á Kempis, got buried prematurely. (Do you know that story—what has breath interred before its time?)

Let's begin with these words of Justin: "On the day named after the sun, all, whether they live in the city or the countryside, are gathered together in unity."[2] I note with surprise that Justin says that folk who live both in and outside the city meet together in unity—despite the usual human pattern in past and present that the city mouse and the country mouse more despise than respect the other's communal rituals and societal morals, more avoid than embrace each other. Is the fact of our various segregations in the contemporary church merely the result of the multiplicity of our options? Or are we failing to achieve what Justin described, the city and country dwellers worshiping in unity?

To Justin's main point in the sentence "Christians assemble on Sunday," I am a Christian, writes Justin, and so I meet with other Christians to worship on Sunday. Twenty centuries later, where I reside in the world, there are fewer practicing Christians than there were during my childhood, but Justin will say to us, "Welcome back to the early days of the church," when there were indeed few of us. And meet together on Sunday.

About Sunday, historians debate myriad questions.[3] Would all Christians have already used the planetary names for the days of the week? Did all Christians in 150 meet on this "sunday"? When did this practice originate? Why? Did the choice of Sunday mean to distinguish Christian practice from Jewish Sabbath observance? Was the meeting in the morning or in the evening of what was a workday? Did the event include a full meal or a symbolic eating and drinking? Did Gentile Christians and Jewish Christians share similar ritual patterns? What prior associations did each assembly of Christians bring to this weekly gathering, and how would these resonances have influenced what occurred? And there are many more such questions. Unearthing the minute hints that are buried in early Christian writings cannot satisfy our immense curiosity about our origins, and I smile to encounter two scholars drawing opposite conclusions from Justin's comment that the readings go on "for as long as there is time," one historian claiming that, granting the need to get to work, there was limited time, and another author countering that, given a kind of Sabbath day, there was plenty of time of worship, a long amount of time.

Justin argues against the maintenance of a Sabbath, as he does of the practice of circumcision, since as a Christian he teaches that such Jewish rituals commanded by the Mosaic law ended with Christ, who established a new covenant. Thus when Justin writes of meeting on Sunday, he is describing an event of worship, not a day of rest. I am convinced by those scholars who say that for most early Christians, Sunday was not a day of rest.[4] It is as if Christians need no Sabbath rest, for as Matthew wrote of Christ, "I will give you rest."[5] This is not to deny that many Americans are overextended in diverse directions and that we ought to rejoice in times of rest as a gift of God's creation. Jewish tradition teaches that rest is a thing, an entity, that God had to create on the seventh day.[6] But I would not connect rest with worship: I know too many parish clergy, church musicians, and Sunday school teachers to contemplate such a suggestion.

I am glad that my Lutheran upbringing was not Sabbatarian. Of course, Connecticut towns in the 1950s did not offer much else to do on Sunday besides worship, and (for Christ's sake!) it did not cross anyone's mind to schedule children's sports activities on a Sunday morning. The stories I heard of my mother's childhood in Lake Wobegon, where not only could one not do the laundry on Sunday, one could not even have Saturday's laundry still hanging out on the line, suggested that such restrictions on Sunday behavior functioned mostly as a checklist for criticizing one's neighbor. And Calvinists discovered that if you forbid work on Sunday, you will end up having to forbid all those other activities that would naturally fill up the empty time. Indeed, even when in 321 Emperor Constantine established Sunday as a day of rest, he had to exclude farmers—that is, the working people upon whose daily tasks the society relies. In truth, isn't it only people of privileged occupations who can take off a day from work?

For Luther, when Christians read the commandments, or indeed anything in the Bible, they are reading through Christian eyeglasses. Thus it is that for contemporary Jews, the commandment to keep the Sabbath means whatever that branch of Judaism says it means, but for Lutherans, the commandment to keep the Sabbath holy means simply this: go to church, and revere the word of God there received. So I go to church. I am drawn to this comment by a Methodist: "Sabbath is more than the absence of work. It is the presence of something that arises when we consecrate a period of time to listen to what is most deeply beautiful, nourishing or true."[7] For me, this "presence" is available at Sunday morning worship. By the way, for Lutherans, the commandment forbidding religious images was laid aside, omitted from Lutheran catechisms, since from earliest times, Christians have found great religious value in the gift of biblical images on their walls and in their texts. It is good to draw Jesus, said Luther and most Lutherans. (But drawing God? Not such a good idea.)

Justin offers us his explanation of why his Christians assemble for worship on Sunday: "We hold this meeting together on the day of the sun since it is the first day, on which day God, having transformed darkness and matter, made the world. On the same day Jesus Christ our savior rose from the dead." Sunday, then, commemorates God's creation of the world and the illumination of its darkness by light, and Sunday stands as always the first day of the week, the outset of each portion of the Christian life, because of the resurrection of Christ. (Please allow into your homes and on your computers only those calendars on which Sunday is the first day of the week, rather than allowing into your consciousness the notion that Sunday is merely the second day of a weekend.) So how do we know if a person is Christian? Many in our time will answer this question by referring to personal belief about Jesus or a private conviction about ultimate values. I prefer outward and objective data—and I don't by "Christian" mean one's generally nice behavior. Rather, we know Christians to be such because, each week, to begin their lives anew, they join with others to praise God for creation and to rejoice in the resurrection of Jesus, which communal gathering impels them, as Justin says, to bring aid to "orphans and widows, those who are in want through disease or through other cause, those who are in prison, and foreigners who are sojourning here."

Some Christians will assemble with others only annually, on Easter Day. In the United States today, church members claim to worship "regularly" when they attend about once a month. I am glad to assemble each Sunday, the first day, which is God's creation of light; it is the Lord's Day, the day of the Lord's resurrection; it is the eighth day, the time of the Spirit, fulfillment time outside of normal time. Thus each Sunday is the community's assembly in the triune God[8]—as good a definition as I have found as the marker for Christian faith and practice.

And what about the acceptability of a midweek Eucharist replacing Sunday, at least if by necessity? I'd suggest Thursday as more christological than, say, Wednesday, since it is on a Thursday that Christians commemorate Jesus' startling practice of footwashing, his prayer for church unity, his hosting the meal of himself, and his arrest—Christ manifest as servant, intercessor, food, and victim—for then and for all time. There is license among Roman Catholics for believers who cannot assemble on Sunday, largely because of work schedules, to attend a Saturday vigil service, an allowance for which I have sympathy. There may be other situations, given the availability of space or of liturgical leadership, for an assembly to sacralize an hour on Saturday at dusk. I remain unconvinced that a transfer into our culture of ancient Hebrew timekeeping, according to which the day begins at sunset, is religiously persuasive. Christmas Eve has supplanted Christmas Day, not because of Jewish tradition, but because of the importance of family festivities and our orgies of gift-giving, and the three-hour Easter Vigil is more like a striking parish retreat than merely the start of Easter Day. Indeed, my observation during twenty-five years of teaching religion at a Roman Catholic university was that although the idea of a Sunday obligation did transfer to Saturday, not much else did: the liturgy functioned more like another Saturday chore than like the inauguration of a new week transformed by the resurrection. Those of you maintaining this practice, I wish you well.

To propose assembling on Sunday as the sign of Christian identity places immense significance on what is often experienced with unsettling disappointment. There is no way that our weekly worship can be everything it is called to be. As the eucharistic prayer in the *Apostolic Constitutions* said it, our worship is always "not as we ought, but as we are able."[9] Yet often what we dish up is nowhere near the feast that we might be able to present. We can take some comfort in that its inadequacy is a sign of a religion of incarnation, in which the divine is, bizarrely, and always only partially, embodied in the human. The mystery of the triune God is manifest, we believers affirm, in this assembly, with these words, these leaders, this music, this bread and wine. But such a faith statement ought not allow us to continue in any silliness or sloppiness, errors or idiocies, essentials omitted or nonsense elaborated. In praise for God's creation, in thanksgiving of Christ's salvation, and in anticipation of the Spirit's final future, we have lots of work to do.

Justin Martyr wrote, "For it is plain that, though beheaded, and crucified, and thrown to wild beasts, and chains, and fire, and all other kinds of torture, we do not give up our confession; but the more such things happen, the more do others and in larger numbers become faithful, and worshipers of God through the name of Jesus. . . . There is not one single human race, whether barbarians, or Greeks, or whatever they may be called, nomads, or vagrants, or herdsmen living in tents, among whom prayers and giving of thanks are not offered through the name of the crucified Jesus."[10] Indeed, we are now back to the days when some Christians, along with Justin, are beheaded. Yet still we are summoned to gather on Sunday. May Justin's life-and-death passion for communal thanksgiving on Sunday be with us all.

2 Chapter

Acclaiming the Trinity with Catherine of Siena

Catherine was born in Siena in 1347 (six hundred years before me) and died on April 29, 1380. She was her mother's twenty-fifth birthing. Although oblivious to our judgments that her eating habits—that is, her not-eating habits—were pathological, she was in many ways a remarkable woman, trespassing many boundaries set out for laywomen in fourteenth-century Italy. (Don't you wonder how many prospective saints we now pacify with drugs?) Understanding herself to be a bride of Christ, she lived so obediently under her husband that, uniting with him, she too died at age thirty-three. Yet while fainting in ecstasy before Christ, she nursed the sick; stood up courageously to family, clergy, and rulers; traveled the countryside with her followers; rebuked the Pope; dictated a masterful theological classic; sent over three hundred letters that asserted her uncompromising opinions; and reconciled quarreling parties. How did she become who she was? Neither credulous piety nor respectful scholarship[1] fully answers this question. In wonder we keep her memory best, not by gawking at her desiccated head in a glass reliquary on a Siena altar, but by joining her in dedication to the Trinity.

For Catherine, all is triune. Although much of her *Dialogue* is composed as if spoken by God the Father, in the conclusion Catherine praises God as "O eternal Trinity! O Godhead!" She calls the Trinity the abyss of charity, the craftsman, that light beyond all light, the angels' food, the garment to cover all nakedness.[2] Aware that no metaphor for God is adequate, she employs opposites in praise of the Trinity—an ever burning yet never consuming fire, and a deep sea. In her ecstatic Prayer 6, offered after her day's communion and transcribed by her followers, she asks the Spirit for power and charity, Christ for protection from evil thoughts and for a loving spirit, and the Father for help in every need.[3] In Prayer 12, the Trinity is power, wisdom, and mercy; light, wisdom, and strength; table, food, and waiter,[4] this last of which I have quoted in one of my compositions.[5] God is one vine with three branches.[6] Repeatedly her praise and petition is addressed to "Eternal Trinity! O high eternal Trinity!"

Over the centuries Christians have defined the ambiguous "image of God" of Genesis 1:27 with whatever human quality they most value: for example, Thomas Aquinas identifies the image of God as rationality, and some theologians as the ability to love. (To complicate our interpretation, we need to account for Genesis 5:3, in which Seth is in Adam's "likeness, according to his image.") However, similar to Augustine, Catherine praises God the Father as memory, the Son as wisdom, and the Spirit as understanding, and this Trinity is not only within God's self, but is God in us.[7] She cried out, "You made us in your image and likeness so that, with our three powers in one soul, we might image your trinity and your unity."[8] I find Catherine's triune image of God more persuasive than a proposal common in our time—God's image as male and female sexuality—a feature that our species shares with animals and even some plants.

Catherine was not the only medieval woman who praised the Trinity. Describing the Trinity as light, person, and fire, Hildegard of Bingen pictured the Trinity with a human figure "the color of a sapphire"—thus a man but not a man—who is doubly encircled with a bright light and glowing fire, "so that the three were one light in one power of potential."[9] In Hildegard's triune eucharistic image, "the Father is understood by the wine, the Son by the bread, and the Holy Spirit by the water."[10] Elisabeth of Schönau wrote, "You see three colors: white, red, and marble. White is the color of Christ's humanity, red represents the Holy Spirit, and the marble color signifies the divinity of the Father."[11] Gertrude of Helfta described herself as a "frail little plant" that the Son of God transforms into a fleur-de-lys, each of her three branches receiving life from one person of the Trinity.[12] For Marguerite Porete, "The Father is eternal substance; the Son is pleasing fruition; the Holy Spirit is loving conjunction."[13] Mechthild of Magdeburg wrote, "The Three Persons sent forth beautifully the beams of light in unison, each of them illumined by the other while remaining utterly one," the Father praised for omnipotence, the Son for infinite wisdom, and the Spirit for full generosity.[14] Julian of Norwich famously described the Trinity as our Father, our Mother, and our Lord: "We are beclosed in the fader, and we are beclosed in the son, and we are beclosed in the holy gost. And the fader is beclosed in us, the son is beclosed in us, and the holy gost is beclosed in us: all mighty, alle wisdom, and alle goodnesse; one God, one lorde."[15] For Julian, because of the Trinity, "alle oure life is in thre."[16] As well, an impressive list of contemporary female theologians find in the Trinity protection from divine patriarchy.[17]

Many churches address most liturgical prayer to the Father, either to replicate the Lord's Prayer or to follow Origen by invoking the Father, through the Son, in the Spirit.[18] This classic pattern functions both rhetorically and theologically, for also the entirety of salvation comes "through the Son" and "in the Spirit." But is it not the case that prayer to the Father grants the first person priority in a Trinity in which the three are meant to be co-equal? It is as if the face of God that matters to one's life is not triune but fatherly. (Check out the shockingly sexist children's dictionary of 1944, in which "father" is defined as "head of the family," and "God" as "our Father in Heaven."[19] Of "mother," the dictionary says, "A mother loves her family.")

When advocating for liturgical reforms, I often invoke the "ramp-cane principle."[20] A town ramped its sidewalk corners to ease the route for wheelchairs, but then persons who used white canes walked out into the traffic. If you are solving one problem, be aware that you are creating another, which you hope is less significant than the one you are addressing. When in recent decades the heaviness of Father was seen as sinking the Christian ship, "father" was often replaced with "God." But herewith you have opened the door to Arius, for if we speak of God, Christ, and the Spirit, there is little sense that Christ and the Spirit are indeed God. Here is another "ramp-cane" example: we sanctify the scriptural language of father and son, but must assert that somehow in this situation, father and son are co-equal.

I find it an invigorating challenge to remain an orthodox believer. Thus, I can still call God Father, Son, and Spirit. However, I react against a rigid claim that this wording is the sole divinely authorized nomenclature, which sounds to me like the biblical literalism that people invoke when they want to substantiate their own preferences. (So we replace Genesis 2-3, which sanctifies the dominance of males, with Genesis 1, which establishes gender equality: both sides of the gender debate quote the Bible in their defense.) First-century Greco-Roman religion knew Jupiter as the Father of fathers, and numerous men of political stature—the Egyptian Pharaohs, Babylonian and Assyrian monarchs, the Roman emperors—were each called "son of god." The Roman Empire even had its own triune divinity: Jupiter; the Emperor, who was son of Jupiter; and the Genius of the Emperor. We Christians borrowed and baptized the religious language of that culture, claiming that the real "son of god" was Jesus of Nazareth and that the only god was "the father" of Jesus. (Please note that capitalization is merely an impermanent linguistic convention.) Yet Christian use of "son of god" has nurtured some consummate nonsense in the history of the church and the piety of believers. So we have ramped the sidewalk: alas for the white canes?

I hope that we can honor the terminology of "Father, Son, and Spirit" with humility, as the best that the church has yet agreed upon, while steadfastly resisting the habit of beating each other up with biblical proof-texts. An initial question: How often in the course of a Sunday liturgy of seventy-five minutes ought "Father, Son, and Spirit" be repeated? Once? Twice? Ten times?

We are called to the continuing theological quest: Are there other trinitarian terms that speak orthodox faith? How would Christians name God when evangelizing in a language that had no word for "father"? Those who assert that the question is closed, the trinitarian room already locked up tight, have left me out in the hallway. The Cappadocian Fathers advocated for the biblical language of Father, Son, and Spirit, rather than for more philosophical categories. Is their argument finally persuasive and definitive? When can the Trinity be the Holy One, the Word, and the Power of the Most High?[21]

Inspired by Catherine, whether in ecstasy (not my capability) or when crafting the options at Sunday worship, let us praise, not merely our denomination's preferred person of the Trinity, but the mystery of the God triune.

With the Orthodox churches, we can address more prayers than the *Agnus Dei* to the second person of the Trinity and more chants than *Veni Creator Spiritus* to the third. We can sometimes adopt the Orthodox pattern in which, despite which person of the Trinity is addressed, many prayers conclude with a sentence of trinitarian praise.[22]

We can consider the triple address used in a eucharistic prayer recently approved by the Anglican Church of Ireland, in which the opening praise is addressed to "Father, Lord of all creation"; the remembrance of the Last Supper is addressed to "Lord Jesus Christ, our redeemer"; and the epiclesis is addressed to "Holy Spirit, giver of life."[23]

We can add glosses to our doctrinal speech. After the words of baptism are spoken over the candidate, the assembly can respond, "Blessed be God, the source of all life, the word of salvation, the power of mercy."[24] We can stop calling the triune name "a formula," as though we are speaking some magical utterance or conducting a chemistry experiment. Thank you, Augustine, for God as Lover, Beloved, Love.[25] How about Father, Son, and Holy Spirit, Source, Servant, and Sanctifier?

Hymns filled with metaphors can carry our trinitarian address. In metaphor, we say A to mean B. In religious discourse, the idea is that a divine A is actually so far beyond precise human verbalization that B is necessary in conveying A. Metaphors embrace the mystery gently. They leave space for new resonances to sneak in. There are traditional metaphorical texts, such as the anonymous eighteenth-century hymn that in four stanzas addresses almighty King, incarnate Word, holy Comforter, and then "great One in Three."[26] Recently Jean Jansen adapted the work of Julian of Norwich into the hymn "Mothering God," who gave me birth, took my form, and nurtures me.[27] Thomas Troeger provides a profusion of trinitarian non-anthropomorphic imagery in "Source and Sovereign, Rock and Cloud."[28]

We can reproduce in our ubiquitous service folders an image of the Trinity. Indeed, we now need not spend a fortune on permanent art in our sanctuaries, since we can enlist the teenagers to monitor computer projections. For such imagery, we can lay aside the traditional old man, young man, and bird. We have the triune icons of Mamre: with all deference to the genius of Andrei Rublev, I prefer the icons titled "The Hospitality of Abraham" (um, and Sarah?) in which the couple attends the three angels, the tablecloth has red stripes, and carrots are at each place.[29] We have Hildegard's triune vision,[30] or the interlocking hand, lamb, and dove, or Patrick's shamrock, or Catherine's three branches of one vine. Such images, each inadequate, offer the assembly at least something threefold to work with.

Catherine concluded her *Dialogue* with these words: "With your light, eternal Trinity, you dispelled the darkness. With that light I sense my soul once again becoming drunk! Thanks be to God! Amen."[31] Let's join Catherine, drinking up the Trinity.

3
Chapter

Speaking of Christ with Ambrose

Ambrose was born in Trier in 340, consecrated bishop of Milan on December 7 in 374—the date on which the church keeps his memory—and died in Milan in 397. As with most of the saints, Ambrose wills us both words to treasure and imitate, even sing, and other words best left on dusty shelves in old libraries and encountered only by graduate students. Online you can see what might be a genuine portrait of him, a fifth-century mosaic in the basilica of St. Ambrogio in Milan, and in the crypt is Ambrose's skeleton, quite a sight, his bones all dressed up in much later episcopal vestments.

Born into a prominent Christian family, Ambrose was well educated in literature and rhetoric and served as governor in the northern capital of the Roman Empire. In a delightful story that is apparently factual, after being popularly acclaimed to fill the episcopal vacancy, he hid away to escape this destiny, but then gave himself up to the will of the people and over eight days was baptized and consecrated. The episode in which he and his followers staged a cathedral sit-in to keep the empress from requisitioning the building for Arian worship can be seen as symbolic of his firm stands in support of the orthodox faith. He is remembered for his care for the poor as well (alas!) as for his harshness against pagans and Jews. Honored as one of the four doctors of the Western church, he was an early promoter of the veneration of the Virgin Mary, and he is praised for having established congregational singing of metrical Latin hymns and the antiphonal chanting of psalms.

Ambrose catechized and baptized Augustine in 387. In his *Confessions,* Augustine wrote that it was not until he had encountered Ambrose's "eloquent sermons" that he began to take Christianity seriously. Augustine, describing those sermons as providing "the sobering intoxication" of the wine of God's word, heard in Ambrose's preaching "various passages in the Old Testament explained most frequently by way of allegory, by which same passages I was killed when I had taken them literally."[1] That is, Ambrose did not rely on literal interpretations of the Bible. Literary scholars would not now refer to Ambrose's technique as allegory, since the term "allegory" designates a sustained comparison between two entities, in which a = A, b = B, c = C, and so on, so that numerous textual details each have specific correspondence to some other meaning, albeit one that is hidden. Neither Ambrose nor I advocate a rigid medieval typology,[2] in which persons and actions in the Old Testament find their legitimacy only in their point-for-point correspondence to the story of Christ, as if two thousand years of history unfolded only as a foil to Christ. Indeed, the term "typology" is bankrupt in our time, its procedure innocent of historical scholarship and its method tending toward anti-Semitism.

The biblical interpretive technique that Ambrose and Augustine shared can be called "figurative." We in the church look for ways to speak of our encounter with Christ, and believers see such figurative possibilities in the Hebrew scriptures, in Greco-Roman religion, in the natural world, here, there: as Augustine said it, Christ meets us everywhere.[3] Such figurative interpretation was standard during the early centuries of Christian hermeneutic. In one of the cubiculums in the catacombs of the Basilica of St. Sebastian, the resurrection that Christ promises is metaphorically depicted by the entire tale of Jonah. (Remember Matthew 12:40?) The prophet tossed into the sea and then being coughed up from the mouth of the sea monster reminds the Christian mourners of their faith in Christ's resurrection. In the Vatican Museum, we see that the stories proclaimed now at the Easter Vigil—the sacrifice of

Isaac, the Israelites' escape across the sea, Jonah emerging from the sea monster, the three children in the fiery furnace[4]—are carved into the front frieze of third-century sarcophagi, as figural images of Christ's own Passover from death to life and in Christian hope for just such salvation for the deceased, who is depicted in the center of the frieze in orans. The metaphoric technique opens the Christian imagination to the treasures of all that is and that can be dreamed, and thus the church sees in surprising places the grace of Jesus Christ.

The human habit of metaphor applies a known mental construct onto a new experience and thus can incorporate the *novum* into the shared body of human consciousness. The twentieth century saw a renewal of philosophical study of metaphor, claiming that the primary and apparently unique characteristic of the human mind is the ability to expand knowledge and communication by likening one thing to another.[5] Metaphor is calling a small gray thing that moves around your desk a mouse. Metaphor is the three-year-old after an hour in the pool looking at her hands and crying out in distress, "Raisin fingers!" Metaphor is the Christian transferring onto Jesus of Nazareth the religious category of "Son of God." And Ambrose was crazy into metaphor.

Examples of Ambrose's perpetual poetic predilection are found in everything he penned. In "The Sacraments," Ambrose interpreted the story of Naaman's being healed from leprosy in the Jordan River as a picture of baptism, since "the water which has the grace of Christ cures."[6] In "The Mysteries," the narrative of Moses sweetening the water of Marah by throwing into the pool a piece of wood is held next to the preaching of "the cross of the Lord," which makes the water of baptism "sweet for grace."[7] In "The Holy Spirit," the story of Gideon's triumph over the Midianites is given value to his hearers because the lamps in the pitchers give "testimony to the passion of the Lord Jesus."[8] Ambrose seems to have enjoyed playing with interpretation. In his lengthy exegesis of Luke's Gospel, Ambrose writes of the parable of the mustard seed, "Let Christ be there where the fruit is. Sow the Lord Jesus; He is a seed when He is grasped, He is a tree when He rises again, a tree overshadowing the world; He is a seed when He is buried in the earth, He is a tree when He is exalted to Heaven."[9] We encounter here Christ as seed of the tree and tree from the seed, and then we move on to yet another metaphor.

Augustine's contemporary Jerome, that preeminent biblical scholar slaving away on accurate Latin translations of the Hebrew and Greek Scriptures, disparaged Ambrose's writing as "flaccid, soft, glistening and cute, painted here and there in exquisite colors."[10] We can hear Jerome shouting, Scrap the similes; stick to the text. So although the surprises of metaphor were kept alive by the medieval mystics, Jerome's preference for historical superstructures became the dominant tradition in much of the West. Embedded in fact-based biblical studies, chronological narration suggests at least to seminarians that the usefulness of a text relies on its historical accuracy. Such an emphasis coordinates with recent centuries of scientific thought, in which only what is fact is valued.

Devout daughter of the Reformation although I am, I must admit that the printing of complete Bibles helped bury Ambrose's patterns of metaphor. In the medieval printed block books that are called *Biblia Pauperum*, Jonah thrown into the sea and arising from the sea monster are set parallel to Christ being laid in the grave and arising from the tomb.[11] In some depictions, Jonah grabs onto a tree to pull himself from the monster's mouth, just as in the parallel picture Christ holds out his victory standard when stepping out of the tomb. But in the printed Bibles of the sixteenth century, illustrations of Jonah are placed in the text of the book of Jonah, and illustrations of Christ's resurrection are alongside the Gospel accounts of Easter. The literalism of the full text has left no room for the metaphoric interplay. The tension woven within truth is smoothed out, laid aside.[12] The mystery in Scripture is replaced with a single intention.[13] When our minds are glued to a prose text, we encounter only one thing at a time. Is one thing all that we can handle?

In our time, when in many churches biblical literalism poses as religious truth, metaphoric understanding of the Bible is more necessary than ever. Augustine wrote about being "killed" by literalist biblical interpretation. Often it is such literalist preaching that slays me, and this from preachers who had to pass courses in critical biblical studies while in seminary and whose church body distances itself from fundamentalist denominations. In the late twentieth century, many theologians have joined with other scholars to discredit an earlier, easier view of the Bible as divinely inspired historical fact. It might be that the primary impetus to literalist biblical teaching is as a sop to the laity, of which I am one, in a time reliant on verifiability. Preachers may worry that it would be sketchy to interpret biblical stories as profound metaphor, without any recourse to facticity. Many of my university students maintained that although Old Testament stories—of which they knew few and cared little—are probably legends, every New Testament account of Jesus is historically accurate, and what is historically accurate is trustworthy. And so despite the Johannine Jesus responding to Martha's anticipation of the final resurrection that he himself is the resurrection, on Lent 5, Year A, some sermons still stress a literal raising of Lazarus and ourselves. Yet in 1928 Harry Emerson Fosdick criticized preachers who assumed "that folk come to church desperately anxious to discover what happened to the Jebusites,"[14] or we might add, to the dead Lazarus.

More honor to Ambrose, who by appointing congregational hymnody put metaphors into the mouths and minds of worshipers. In Ambrose's morning hymn "Splendor paternae gloriae," Christ is the light, the sun, the dawn, and thus the dawn expresses the double meaning of both nature and grace.[15] In his Advent hymn translated "Savior of the Nations, Come," Ambrose employs the cosmic imagery of God's realm above our earthly planet as a metaphor for Christ's incarnation.[16] What was it that turned so many contemporary composers of hymns toward delight in metaphor? Was it the church's rediscovery of the poetry of the psalms? Was it weariness with medieval doctrine? Did the Spirit of God open up the hymnals so that the proud waves of the sea could pour in once more? Dozens of hymn texts composed in recent decades are masterpieces of metaphor. In "You, Lord, Are Both Lamb and Shepherd,"[17] hymnwriter Sylvia Dunstan relativized each metaphor for Christ by pairing it to its opposite, and in the process offers us twenty-eight images to sing. In the final stanza of "Alleluia! Jesus Is Risen," Herbert Brokering shouts out eight images, one after another, metaphors for the resurrection.[18]

In preaching on the Good Samaritan, Ambrose said that the Samaritan is Christ, his words are medicines, and he is even the beast who carries us on his shoulders. The denarii are "perhaps the two Testaments, upon which have been stamped the image of the Eternal King, by whose price our wounds were healed."[19] In the mind of Ambrose, both the Samaritan's pack animal and the coins of the Roman Empire can show forth Christ, one metaphor always beckoning another, the imagery giving meaning to otherwise inconsequential details in the biblical narrative.

Let's consider Matthew's report of a miraculous star. What use has this star in our time? I suggest that seeing Matthew's star as a metaphor for Christ is a gift. This interpretation lends contemporary value to the tale of the Magi, making of the star something other than a bizarre supernatural heavenly body that may only distract our attention away from the actual universe that God created. Thanks to Ambrose, who preaching on Epiphany said, "This Star is the way, and the way is Christ: for in the mystery of the incarnation Christ is a star."[20]

May his bones sing.

4
Chapter

Invoking the Spirit
with Symeon the New Theologian

S ymeon, the Byzantine mystic and poet, has been named by the Eastern church "the new theologian." The Eastern tradition confers the honorific "theologian" to only three persons—the evangelist John, Gregory of Nazianzus, and Symeon—the title indicating their eminence as Orthodox authorities who spoke from personal experience of God. Yet in an ecclesial tradition in which what is new is suspect, the ambiguity in the title also registers a traditional uneasiness with especially Symeon's novel teaching that all the baptized are capable of mystical experiences of the Holy Spirit.

Born in 949 into a noble family residing near the Black Sea in Asia Minor, he was educated for a career in the court, and for some years enjoyed the wild life. In his twenties, the mystic entered a monastic community, after having taken on the name of his revered spiritual guide, Symeon the Pious, a lay monk who as one of those Orthodox "holy fools" was severely criticized for bizarre behaviors such as walking around naked. (Church history is not boring.) By 980, at the age of thirty-one, Symeon had become the abbot of the monastery of St. Mamas in Constantinople and became well known for delivering lectures to the monks based on his mystical encounters and for stressing the primary role of the Spirit in Christian life. Meanwhile he was harshly judged for his reverence for the elder Symeon, for his excessively strict monastic regimen, and for his emphasis on personal mystical experience, which was seen in the headquarters in Constantinople as a threat to established hierarchical authority. In 1005, after twenty-five years as abbot, he resigned and later was exiled, and although recalled, he remained in the small monastic community that he had formed, away from the centers of political and ecclesiastical life. He spent his last decades perfecting his collection of fifty-eight hymns and died on March 12, 1022.

For Symeon, it was the believers' participation in the Holy Spirit that led to their divinization—that Eastern Christian emphasis on being gathered into the divine life. (I judge the English word "divinization" as more accurate and less open to misunderstanding than its synonym "deification" at expressing what the Orthodox tradition is getting at.) Genuine Christian faith, as opposed to empty religious ritual, required one's cooperation with the Holy Spirit and led inevitably toward the goal of personal sanctity. Symeon is the first in Christian history to be recorded as speaking of the baptism of the Holy Spirit as a second personal experience separate from one's first sacramental baptism, and every Christian, he taught, was capable of conscious direct experiences of the Holy Spirit. Just as in the Eastern tradition it is the power of the Holy Spirit that transforms the eucharistic elements of bread and wine, so also believers themselves are inhabited by the divine Spirit, to become what God intends for the whole creation: to be vessels of divinity.

Symeon described his mystical experiences as of joyous yet overwhelming light. In one example of Symeon's heightened rhetoric, he listed many rituals and disciplines of Christian practice and concluded: "So if I walk along [these practices] for a thousand years, and do not reach the light, which is the Holy Spirit, who proceeds from the Father, and through the Son enlightens every man who comes, yet if at my departure from this life I am found to be still in the darkness, what have I gained? . . . The grace of the Holy Spirit is the cause of our union with Christ, and it is not possible for anyone not conscious of having the Holy Spirit dwelling within him to have fellowship with Christ."[1] He explained that "without the Spirit there is neither the Father nor his Son."[2] His much quoted—and usually shortened—"Invocation to the Holy Spirit" calls the Spirit true light, eternal life, hidden mystery, nameless treasure, ineffable reality, inconceivable person, endless bliss, non-setting sun, non-tarnishing crown, purple of the great king our God, crystalline cincture, studded with precious stones, inaccessible sandal (!) . . . my breath and my life, consolation of my poor soul, my joy, my glory, my endless delight.[3] His hymns, written in poetic meter and rhyme with eight, twelve, or fifteen syllables per line, are filled with lush descriptions of the Holy Spirit. Symeon wrote of the Spirit,

> He is really the only tree of life, He who is planted
> in whatever earth that is, in the souls of whatever men
> or takes roots in their hearts, at once
> He brings forth this resplendent Paradise,
> adorned by all types of beautiful plants, trees and various
>   fruits,
> covered with flowers and with thousands of sweet-smelling
>   lilies.[4]

Symeon urged those believers who have not had such a mystical experience to trust the testimony of those who have and to open themselves up for such transformation.[5]

Although there seems to be no connection between the writings of Symeon and the twentieth-century rise of Pentecostalism, both expressed a preference for personal experience over ecclesiastic authority and a criticism of empty formalized religion. Thus, not surprisingly, both led to censure from some established church structures and the wariness of mainstream Christianity. Symeon saw the baptism of the Holy Spirit as evidenced in the gift of tears, a medieval phenomenon shared by various mystics. In our time, on January 1, 1901, while a student at a Kansas college, Agnes Ozman expressed her second baptism in the form of glossolalia, an event which led soon afterward to the famous Azusa Street Revival. Both overflowing with tears and speaking in tongues are signs of uncontained personal emotion.

I must say that neither I nor any Christian whom I know well has experienced some second Baptism of the Spirit, and so in this way I stand at a considerable yet respectful distance from Symeon. Yet the power of the Spirit is not held captive to personal experience nor expressed solely through individual testimonies. In this, as in many other situations, the church of the ages is always wading through a swamp along the shoreline: where lies authority, in individual testimony or in church tradition? What is the process, and how many centuries does it take, for an extraordinary personal experience to become grafted into and thus influence future growth in church tradition? How do we know who has the Spirit: Savonarola? Luther? How can the churches of each century find where to stand between the reckless left and the rigid right?

In recent decades, many feminist Christians have revivified their worship with additional praise to and petition for the Holy Spirit, in part to balance the Western attention to God as Father and as Son. Already we see this in a nineteenth-century prayer by Christiana Rossetti, in which she applies the standard images for the Spirit to specific petitions:

> Holy Spirit,
> as the wind is thy symbol, so forward our goings,
> as the dove, so launch us heavenwards,
> as water, so purify our spirits,
> as a cloud, so abate our temptations,
> as dew, so revive our languor,
> as fire, so purge out our dross.[6]

In what many of us recognize as the preeminent theological proposal in our time exploring the Christian feminine divine, the role of "Spirit-Sophia" is granted precedence over

"Jesus-Sophia" and "Mother-Sophia," since it is the Spirit who brings God to humans and humans to God.[7] The practice of referring to especially the Spirit with the female pronoun has spread to many worshiping assemblies, and it is apparent that this is an empowering linguistic technique for some Christians. For me, the explicit sexuality implied when American English refers to God as either "he" or "she" is ultimately a barrier that obstructs the journey toward divine mystery, and thus when speaking of God, I avoid he, she, and it.[8] Happily, prayer is addressed to God as "you," and thus need not rely on third-person pronouns. But I am grateful for texts at worship that recognize, praise, and petition the Spirit.

Despite an annual blowout on Pentecost Sunday, the churches I attend direct far less than one-third of their worship on or to the Spirit. Indeed, the classic Western tradition maintained that supplication must be directed solely to the Father, whom Symeon usually called "the Creator." Eastern prayer, by contrast, weaves the three persons of the Trinity together into a single brocade of praise and petition. It is as if the Eastern Oneness of God disregards those Western editors who strive to delineate the divine Threeness. So here are some questions concerning the place of the Spirit in the classic *ordo* of Sunday worship—Gathering, Word, Meal, and Sending.

Can the Gathering rites more fully honor the Spirit's role in bringing together the Body of Christ this week? Can the assembly face the font to honor the pouring out of the Spirit on all the baptized? At the Word, the Presbyterian tradition advocates a prayer for illumination before the readings, and some of these prayers invoke the Holy Spirit. Is such a practice one that all of us might adopt? I would much prefer a prayer entreating the Spirit's presence in the word than the more common practice of the preacher beginning the sermon with a prayer, which (alas!) always suggests to me the possibility of a less-than-adequate sermon preparation. Can our intercessions beg the Spirit to come into the earth itself, as well as onto the world's governments? (As a university student in the 1960s hired to craft the intercessory prayers for campus worship, I was challenged by the chaplain concerning the appropriateness of having asked God's Spirit to descend upon the Soviet Union. Could a communist nation receive the Spirit? That was the cold war for you.) Do we invoke the Spirit as healer for the sick and suffering? Ought we pray more regularly for the gifts of the Holy Spirit to find expression in the lives of the faithful? Most eucharistic prayers ask for the Spirit's entry into the bread and wine. Ought the epiclesis be extended to include the sharing of the Communion, the participants themselves, even the faithful who are absent on this Sunday? How often ought the Sending reiterate the power of the Spirit for our lives during the coming week?

Candles are probably on or around the altar. When and how are the candles lit? Do they suggest the presence of the Spirit? If not, why have them? When would dozens—hundreds—of votive candles, positioned all around the room, be a reminder of the Spirit in our baptism? Will the baptism of even infants testify, not merely to the cuteness of newborns, but also to the transformative mystery of the divine Spirit in human life? Does our worship make clear when else, besides confirmation and ordination, the Spirit descends on the faithful? Can our artists ensure that the imagery of the Spirit's fire embroidered on our paraments be suggestive of more than a small can of Sterno? Are bolts of flowing red fabric, twelve or twenty feet long, more suggestive of the uncontrollable Spirit than is felt glued onto canvas?

In the Nicene Creed, it is the Spirit who is the giver of life, and many of our hymns celebrate this Spirit. In *Veni Creator Spiritus*, the ninth-century hymn perhaps penned by Rhabanus Maurus, the Spirit, the heavenly dove who restores the creation to God's intent, is named Comforter, fount of life, fire of love, the soul's anointing, light, love, might, protection from the foe, divine peace, strength, guide, and teacher of the faith. Does our version of the thirteenth-century *Veni Sancte Spiritus* include its remarkable petitionary stanzas? Madeleine Forell

Marshall's striking translation of one of Paul Gerhardt's seventeenth-century hymns calls the Spirit "Sweet delight, most lovely, shining faithful friend . . . source of life and every blessing, consolation, ever ready, everlasting, vital breath."[9] Recently, hymn writers have provided us with yet more images of the Spirit: James K. Manley gave us the "Spirit of gentleness" and the "Spirit of restlessness,"[10] and Shirley Erena Murray describes the loving Spirit as "like a mother . . . like a father . . . friend and lover."[11] In Herman Stuempfle's "God of Tempest," the Spirit is seen in the whirlwind of Pentecost, in blazing fire, in earthquake and thunder,[12] while Carl Daw likens the Spirit's coming to the "murmur of the dove's song."[13] Note the opposites in these hymns, as the poets plead for both the transcendence and immanence of the Spirit, divine epiphany both beyond and within. Can we sing these hymns more than once a year? Perhaps at least one each month?

In his discourse "On Partaking of the Holy Spirit," Symeon wrote, more simply than is usual in his style, "The door is the Son. The key to the door is the Holy Spirit."[14] The key has been given us: let's use it more than was our wont.

5
Chapter

Renouncing the Devil with Perpetua

Christian tradition remembers that on March 7, 203, the noblewoman and nursing mother Perpetua, a slave Felicity, and several other Christians were martyred by being thrown to the wild beasts in the amphitheater in Carthage, North Africa. One redactor of *The Passion of Saints Perpetua and Felicitas* notes that when entering the arena, Perpetua fixed her hair, not wanting a disheveled appearance to suggest that she was grieving her martyrdom.[1] The designated mad cow was unsuccessful in killing Perpetua, who in the end assisted "the novice gladiator" in cutting her own throat. She has been commemorated since at least 354, and by the late fourth century, Augustine complained that the account of Perpetua's martyrdom, read aloud in the assembly, was being revered as highly as was Scripture. By the sixth century, Perpetua, called in chapter 18 of the *Passion* "a wife of Christ and darling of God," was named in the Roman canon.

Most scholars concur that while in prison, the well-educated bilingual Perpetua composed her memoirs, sections of which became chapters 3–10 of the *Passion*, thus making her the only known Christian woman to write in her own name before the fourth century. Given that there is no record of any role she played in the Christian community while alive, her fame relies solely upon the affecting narration in the *Passion*. (Note: luminous prose prevails.) Some current scholars do question the historical reliability of the account. They dismiss any essentialist gender identification of the prose style of chapters 3–10 and, noting the parallels between the narrative and the biblical passages Joel 2:28-29 and Acts 2:17-18, propose instead that the *Passion*, including the purported memoir, is a deliberate literary production from somewhat later than 203.[2]

This debate about authorial authenticity is not what interests me on Sunday morning. Rather, I am caught by the references to the devil. In chapter 3, Perpetua's father advances "arguments of the devil"; in chapter 10, Perpetua speaks of her upcoming "fight with the devil"; in chapter 20, it is the devil that prepared for Perpetua a mad cow; and in chapter 21, "the unclean spirit," that is, the devil, is in the gladiator. Most memorably, in the first of Perpetua's four visions, she steps on the head of the serpent[3]—most publications render the Latin *draco* as dragon—as she ascends the ladder to encounter the white-haired shepherd. Whether translated as serpent or dragon, the creature recalls Genesis 3:15 and then Revelation 12:9, "the great dragon, that ancient serpent, who is called the Devil and Satan, the deceiver of the whole world."

Historians of Christianity trace this devil back to dualist ancient Near Eastern religion. Religious systems have found a supernatural devil and its subsidiary demons to be feasible ways to explain the endless conflict between good and evil. (You might note that I do not assign the devil a gendered pronoun, neither "he," despite usual practice, nor "she," despite the medieval depictions of the serpent in Eden with a face identical to that of Eve.)[4] The early classical theory of the atonement appropriated this mythology of evil: on the cross, Christ was battling against the devil, and in his resurrection, Christ demonstrated his triumph over Satan.[5] Later in Christian history, despite the psychological usefulness of Satan, fiercely monotheistic theologians demoted the devil, stressing instead the devilish self within each human person with which our baptism contends.

According to Jewish tradition, Uriel, one of the four archangels who held up the throne of God, was in charge of punishing evil, thus providing an indirect way for God to effect discipline on the people. Christianity did not admit Uriel into its picture of heaven. Instead, the devil took on this role, coming to be in service to God for the purposes of divine chastisement. One recent study cites both Enlightenment philosophy and eighteenth-century Protestantism, by ridiculing medieval Roman Catholic stories of demons and miracles, as bolstering widespread dismissal of the devil.[6] However, we now witness the rise of after-school Satan clubs, and some contemporary Christians maintain that only a literal acceptance of biblical talk of Satan and exorcisms can save the church from trivializing the terrifying power of evil.[7]

Not the devil, nor "Satan," nor the serpent, nor the dragon receives any mention in our creeds. The apocalyptic adventures of the dragon in the book of Revelation have no place in the ecumenical three-year lectionary. I do not think that there exists such a being that embodies sin and evil and that expends its supernatural energy luring humans into its hellish realm. But perhaps the majority of Christians do, and the serpent does slither around on Sunday morning, if not in our sanctuaries, then outside in the churchyard. So let us trace the serpent's movements, in baptismal renunciations, in the lectionary, and in hymnody.

Most baptismal rites include renunciations, a remnant of ancient exorcisms. The baptismal instructions of John Chrysostom tell the catechumens that "even if the demon be fierce and cruel, he must withdraw from your hearts with all speed" upon hearing the exorcism; and "What are the pomps of the devil? Every form of sin, spectacles of indecency, horse racing, gatherings filled with laughter and abusive language . . . tokens, amulets, and incantations."[8] (Laughter is as bad as incantations?) I smiled at another of Chrysostom's comments: "Again there are chariot races and satanic spectacles in the hippodrome, and our congregation is shrinking."[9] Scolding the gathered assembly about lowered church attendance has venerable history.

A recent ecumenical liturgical reform has been to schedule baptisms within the regular Sunday worship. No longer shunted off to a side chapel, the rite of baptism invites all believers who are present to celebrate the sacrament and strengthen their baptismal identity. In the church I attend, the renunciation includes these three questions: "Do you renounce the devil and all the forces that defy God? Do you renounce the powers of the world that rebel against God? Do you renounce the ways of sin that draw you from God?"[10] The Anglican tradition also includes both reference to the devil and its demythologizing: "Do you renounce Satan and all the spiritual forces of wickedness that rebel against God?"[11] Characteristically, the Orthodox churches amplify the question: "Dost thou renounce Satan, and all his Angels, and all his works, and all his service, and all his pride?"[12] In some denominations, specific reference to the devil is omitted. "Trusting in the gracious mercy of God, do you turn from the ways of sin and renounce evil and its power in the world?"[13] Each of the Roman Catholic options includes the specific naming of Satan: "Do you reject Satan and all his works and all his empty promises?" or "Do you reject Satan?" or "Do you reject Satan, father of sin and prince of darkness?"[14] The baptism volume of *Alternative Futures for Worship* included this wording: "Do you renounce Satan and all Satan's works and all Satan's empty promises?"[15] By the way, I participated in that collaboration and recall that one of our number urged that Satan's name be omitted from the renunciations. (Don't we all wonder about revision committees: who won this debate, who won the next one?) For what it's worth, the anthropologist and faithful Episcopalian Margaret Mead, in preparatory discussion of the 1979 *Book of Common Prayer*, urged that reference to Satan remain in the rite for baptism.[16]

In the shared Western lectionary, the devil occasionally shows its face. On Maundy Thursday, the devil has put into the heart of Judas to betray Jesus. On Easter 7, Year A, the devil prowls around like a roaring lion. On the Sunday of Matthew's parable of the wheat and the weeds, the allegory blames the devil for having sowed the weeds, and on the Sunday of Luke

10:16, Jesus remarks, "I watched Satan fall from heaven . . . I have given you authority . . . over all the power of the enemy." Our list might include the stories of exorcisms. But the devil comes into its own on Lent 1. Although Mark says only that Jesus was "tempted by Satan," the legend grew, as legends do, and both Matthew and Luke narrate the three-act adventure during which Jesus rejects Satan's temptation to employ messianic power in such a way as to avoid the cross. (I recall in middle school encountering Edward Everett Hale's 1863 short story "A Man Without a Country," a brilliantly crafted piece of fiction that when first published resulted in countless Americans appealing to the president to pardon a man who had never existed outside the story. It seems that both Matthew and Luke, in elaborating Mark's few words, appreciated the power of narrative.) In Year A, in accord with the intertextuality of the Scriptures, the lectionary pairs the temptation of Jesus with that of Eve and Adam in Genesis 3. I fear that the parallel provided by these two biblical passages has strengthened, if not our faith in Christ's victory over evil, then merely the traditional Western blaming of woman for evil.

I listen for the devil also in hymns. Texts with rhythm and rhyme cement themselves into our minds, and we find ourselves repeating these lines while grocery shopping on Tuesday. The vast majority of our hymns do not mention the devil, but many churches sing Martin Luther's late medieval "A Mighty Fortress Is Our God," in which believers are situated on a battlefield, with a champion fighting with and for us against the adversary Satan. In a recent translation of this classic, Satan is said to "rant and rage."[17] Also in Luther's Easter hymn *Christ Lag in Todesbanden*, "Satan cannot harm us."[18] In Rhabanus Maurus's eighth-century *Veni Creator Spiritus*, the Latin phrase *hostem repellas longius* is variously translated: in my hymnal, the line is "Keep far from us our cruel foe."[19] According to the well-known Christmas carol "God Rest You Merry, Gentlemen," Christ is born "to save us all from Satan's power when we were gone astray."[20] In the nineteenth century, the devout Presbyterian layman Horatio Spafford, having endured repeated tragedies, wrote "When Peace, Like a River," and included the line "Though Satan should buffet, though trials should come, . . . it is well with my soul."[21] May I here praise those churches that provide hymnals in the pews, so that sitting there before worship begins, any interested believer can peruse the hymns, without recourse to the liturgy planner's personal computer.

And so, as we baptize our catechumens, proclaim and preach the lectionary's choices, and sing our hymns, we ask: how is the best way to articulate the stranglehold of sin and the immensity of evil? Although I now advocate a weekly printing or projection of images from Christian history or contemporary artists to complement the lectionary, Christian art has been inadequate when depicting the menace and horror of evil. The West has drawn Satan as a humanoid with distorted body parts, pointed ears, bat wings, a long tail, raptor talons, dark red or black skin, and an obscene rear end. Much of this medieval depiction provided the template for the early generation of Hollywood's evil aliens.[22] And what is sillier than monstrous lizards are the film industry's exorcisms, with levitating virgins vomiting green slime. (If you have forgotten *The Exorcist*, view it again.)

The inquiry about whether literalizing biblical texts strengthens or diminishes their power applies of course not only to references to the devil. That the Gospel according to John narrates Jesus' first miracle as his producing over a hundred and fifty gallons of wine strikes me as more christologically kerygmatic if it is proclaimed as metaphor, rather than as Jesus' biography. Here are some questions addressed to us Sunday worshipers who do not accept the existence of a supernatural devil: How do we ensure that we do not overlook the devastating might of evil, substituting instead only social problems and personal growth experiences? Does explicit reference to the devil give baptismal renunciations more potency? Is the name "Satan" the best that we have? Or does such naming of evil render the text childish, perhaps even ridiculous? Ought our lectionaries edit away some of their references to the devil? Should we keep singing ancient hymn texts? Who is given charge of the translation of historic texts? Does Sunday worship not concern itself with demythologizing, but rather present both a realistic devil and an inspired metaphor? (I have wondered about whether we might identify different denominations, not by their historic quarrels, but by which biblical images they literalize and which they do not.)

That the Bible gives us various ways to word the horror—serpent, dragon, Satan, the devil, the demons—is a gift, since seeing evil from different angles increases our vision and thwarts the temptation to turn story into fact. Yet I have never been as devastated by evil occasioned by baptismal references to the devil as I am nearly nightly while watching a half-hour of BBC World News. Can our liturgy say "evil" with enough malignancy to make necessary Christ's salvation?[23]

"I am a Christian," calls out Perpetua. Fixing her hair as she faces the devil, she faces us as well. Standing with her, let us rejoice in the Christian baptismal sign of God's power over evil and, hopeful in that promise, find ourselves able, as was Perpetua, to treat the serpent's head as a step stool to God.

6
Chapter

Confessing Sin with Martin Luther

T he theologian Martin Luther was an Augustinian friar, professor of Scripture, ecclesiastical critic, excommunicant, imperial outlaw, Bible translator, best-selling author, hymnwriter, polemicist, evangelical preacher, conservative liturgical consultant, husband of an ex-nun, father of six children, and progenitor of Protestantism. He penned both luminous theology for the baptized—the essay *The Freedom of a Christian*—and scathing condemnation of those he opposed, particularly the Jews and the pope—and yet by 1529 was stating that he'd rather drink blood with the pope than wine with the Swiss. Born into a medieval world, dying in the Renaissance on February 18, 1546, Luther stands in everyone's way. We cannot go around him; we must somehow get through him. I am grateful that many of us are undertaking that journey together. It is Luther's call to confess our sins that we still hear half a millennium later and that deserves our consideration on Sunday morning.

The young man Martin Luther was, by our therapeutic standards, overly obsessed with personal guilt, exaggerating his own offenses, terrified of divine judgment, and critical of the church's procedures for offering forgiveness to the faithful. Beginning with his 1517 Latin academic theses proposing a discussion of the church's rituals of penance and popularized with his 1518 German "Sermon on Indulgences and Grace" and his 1519 German essay "The Sacrament of Penance,"[1] Luther directed much of his early career to questions concerning sin and confession: Were Christians capable of sincere contrition? Could Christians actually know their own sins? In what ways did God punish us for our sins, and what might the church do about it? How ought indulgences to function? What was the relationship between the church's rituals of penance and God's free gift of forgiveness? Were not the church's sacraments to be in the business of proclaiming the Gospel? Who held the keys of the kingdom? Although Luther's ecclesial context and methods of argument were quite different from ours, he was, with us, addressing myriad questions about human sin and divine forgiveness and the ways that the liturgy might best address these issues.

I was raised on a conservative branch of the Lutheran tree. In 1960, as part of eighth-grade confirmation instruction, I was urged to prepare for Holy Communion, which was offered four times a year on Sunday evenings (don't tell me the church never changes), by repeating a set of "Christian Questions with Their Answers," which began with this exchange: "Do you believe that you are a sinner? Yes, I believe it; I am a sinner."[2] Nothing resembling this private preparatory ritual is alive in the Lutheran church of which I am now a member. But sin remains a big deal among Lutherans, a foundational principle. Some years ago, I attended the Sunday liturgy at twenty-five different Lutheran churches to discover which ones used the worship materials advocated by our national church, and thus would regularly include a confession of sin in their service, and which used some other worship form. I discovered that most of the freelancers not only did not include a rite of confession of sin, but did not mention sin during the entire event. Yet despite those renegade congregations, most Lutheran churches for much of the church year participate in a ritual exchange of confession and absolution.

In this Lutherans are joined by Roman Catholics, Episcopalians, Methodists, and Presbyterians, among whom the primary worship resources for Sunday include some adaptation of medieval sacramental penance. Rituals of private confession and absolution may be in some ways ideal, but we liturgists know that our imaginings about perfect penitential rites crash into the reality of our cultural situation: the vast majority of Christians do not seek private absolution. Sunday worship is what we have. And although what is called the Human Potential Movement suggests that inculcating a regret for personal sinfulness diminishes what people can be, given the great good of high self-esteem, most of the Christian church maintains that liturgy must articulate truth; that such truth about sin is finally, if not welcome, at least wholesome for each person; that feelings of guilt may have nothing to do with accepting personal culpability for sin; and that the human tendency to blame everyone else for everything is not a worthy path forward.

Teaching religion at a Roman Catholic university, I asked the students whether a two-year-old snatching a toy from another toddler was sinning: no, they all called out. Was an eight-year-old hitting a friend sinning? No. Well, how old would you have to be to sin? An eighteen-year-old called out: "Twenty." Such late adolescent attitudes left me wondering whether those Americans who attend worship actually consider themselves sinners. Ordained clergy and pastoral counselors tell me: yes, they do. People regret their actions, are angered at themselves for consistently bad conduct, are guilty over a secret past, try to erase memory of failure. Indeed, it seems to me that people who live aware of world news and alert to their own behavior are called to face the staggering horror of evil, the inescapable force of sin, the bitter facts of their own past, the monsters hiding near the door, the serpent residing within. Since Christians believe that sin is in the first place before the face of God, the baptized ought to have occasion to acknowledge their sin before God, hear the words of divine mercy, and accept the challenge of baptismal grace. And, to repeat, Sunday worship is what we have.

To confess sin is to acknowledge the truth of the human distance from God, to articulate self-awareness concerning the flawed human condition. In the confession of sin, we ritualize our belief that we are not divine little deities running around. We are not even by nature buddy-buddy with God. As the current Lutheran liturgical resources word it, "We are captive to sin and cannot free ourselves" and "We have turned from you and given ourselves into the power of sin."[3] Sin is the pervasive condition of the human species: it is not mainly the province of men; it is not largely the sphere of women.[4] Some persons try to save themselves by brandishing their own power, while others try to escape responsibility by claiming their own helplessness. Sigmund Freud was Lutheran about this: we are all sick sick sick, and there is no way out; there are only ways to try to deal with it. For Christians, one such way is located in the Sunday assembly. As a contemporary Lutheran pastor wrote about confession and absolution, "When I first experienced it—the part where everyone in church stands up and says what bad people they are, and the pastor, from the distance of the chancel and the purity of her white robe says, 'God forgives you'—I thought it was hogwash. . . . Eventually the confession and absolution liturgy came to mean everything to me. It gradually began to feel like a moment when truth was spoken, perhaps for the only time all week, and it would crush me and then put me back together."[5]

"Confession of sin" is not the same thing as "a confession of sins." A common practice for this ritual is to substitute for the theological category of sin a list of sins, specific infractions, examples of rotten behavior. Often these texts are informed by the week's lectionary readings, and some are thoughtfully crafted. In their extensive liturgical support for the Revised Common Lectionary, Presbyterians provide for each week a Call to Confession, a Prayer of Confession, and the Declaration of Forgiveness appropriate to the biblical readings.[6] Meta-phors—"Our lives bear the scars of sin: bind up our wounds"[7]—are useful. But I hesitate when confessions particularize sin into sins. Sometimes these texts are worded in the plural—"we" have done this and that—although the intention is in fact "I." How often will a worshiper rightly think, Well, for heaven's

sake, I'm not guilty of that! At the Lutheran university I attended in the 1960s, when one thousand students attended the
impressive Sunday Eucharist, three hundred a daily chapel
service, the truly devout also a Wednesday evening Eucharist
and evening dormitory devotions, we were given a text in
which we confessed "the poverty of our worship." As college
students, we were guilty of lots of sins, but the poverty of our
worship was not one of them.

Our churches need continual reflection about whether a
creedal statement of human sinfulness and the reception of
divine forgiveness can be adapted to include a list of individual
sins. One manual for improving congregational prayer makes
the important point that communally reading aloud an unfa-
miliar text listing this and that sin could well become no more
than a mechanical exercise in literacy, rather than a heartfelt
occasion for confession.[8] One technique for individualizing a
general confession is to maintain substantial silence after the
call to confession: "substantial" does not mean ten seconds,
but rather a lengthy heavy space for genuine examination of
one's conduct.

A stunning confession of sin profound in its comprehensive-
ness is the *Ashamnu*, the shorter alphabetical confession in the
Jewish Yom Kippur service, first recorded in about 860 by
Rabbi Amram. Here is one English translation:

> We abuse, we betray, we are cruel. We destroy, we embitter,
>   we falsify.
> We gossip, we hate, we insult. We jeer, we kill, we lie.
> We mock, we neglect, we oppress. We pervert, we quarrel,
>   we rebel.
> We steal, we transgress, we are unkind. We are violent, we
>   are wicked, we are xenophobic.
> We yield to evil, we are zealots for bad causes.[9]

According to this masterful text, we humans are all guilty of
everything; we cause sin, we share in one another's sin, we
confess each other's sin. Using this prayer, we return like chil-

dren to the basics, to our ABCs.[10] When asked why the Yom Kippur confession was arranged in alphabetical order, one rabbi replied: "If it were otherwise we should not know when to stop beating our breasts. For there is no end to sin, and no end to the awareness of sin, but there is an end of the alphabet."[11] The alphabet serves itself up as metaphor, the rudiments of human language become the method of prayer.

Some Christians question whether clergy can proclaim absolution to a motley crew of worshipers, perhaps many of whom are not genuinely repentant. Thus some people advocate that an absolution be replaced with a benign wish: "May God forgive your sins." Yet the Sunday situation is no different from private confession, when honesty or contrition may be absent. And at least a Lutheran would assert that as each communicant is offered the body and blood of Christ, the meal brings with it forgiveness. Just as the communion ministers must trust to the piety of each communicant or to the boundless mercy of God, so the presider can announce forgiveness to the whole gang—a ritual proclamation that itself may call penitents to faith.

Given the magnitude and pervasiveness of sin, one could argue that a dialogue in which in one minute we say that we have sinned and then in the next minute we receive forgiveness does more pastoral harm than spiritual good. But consciousness of sin actually pervades the Sunday liturgy. Worshipers can be shown that in the texts of the *Gloria in Excelsis*, the Nicene and Apostles' Creeds, and the *Agnus Dei* we each week plead for God's mercy on our sin. One suggestion for occasionally lengthening and intensifying the exchange of confession and absolution would be to replace a spoken text with a hymn pleading for forgiveness. From the fifth century we have Synesius of Cyrene's "Lord Jesus, Think on Me"[12]; from Luther, his hymnic version of Psalm 130, "Out of the Depths"[13]; from the seventeenth-century Slovak Jiří Tranovský, "Your Heart, O God, Is Grieved"[14]; from the ex-slaver John Newton, "Amazing Grace"[15]; from an Anglican become Roman Catholic, "There's a Wideness in God's Mercy"[16]; from a twentieth-century Roman Catholic man, an adaptation of the parable of the prodigal son, "Our Father, We Have Wandered"[17]; from a twentieth-century Anglican woman, "Forgive Our Sins as We Forgive"[18]; and from the Maori people, "Son of God, Whose Heart Is Peace."[19] I do not confess my sin alone, but with centuries of the penitent around the world: does that help the ritual to find its meaning?

By the way, the Council of Nicaea forbade kneeling on Sunday.

Each year on February 18, I hope that Christians can thank God for at least some of what Luther accomplished. He became disgracefully judgmental as he aged. But Luther's final words, measured and humble, found by his deathbed, were "We are beggars, this is true." Note the "we." May his confession find expression in our Sunday worship.

7
Chapter

Welcoming All Genders
with Margaret Fell

Margaret Fell has now outlasted the period of history during which she was described solely as the help-mate of her second husband, the Quaker George Fox. Born in 1614 into the landed English gentry, she was married for nearly thirty years to Thomas Fell, a prominent justice of the peace and a member of Parliament, during which time she carried out numerous responsibilities at her estate Swarthmoor Hall and throughout the wider British society. She bore eight children. In 1652, as a consequence of her having hosted at her home the itinerant Quaker preacher George Fox, she became convinced—the Quaker term for conversion. Her husband died in 1658, and after eleven years as a wealthy widow, she was married to Fox until his death in 1691, joining with him to further the Quaker movement. For her procreative leadership role during the early years of the Religious Society of Friends, she is honored as the Mother of Quakerism.

Exacerbated by the social instability in England before, during, and after the Civil War, laws forbidding religious associations outside of the established state church meant that many of her fellow Quakers were imprisoned, and she dedicated much energy to their care and toward their release. Fell herself spent over four years imprisoned for hosting Quaker meetings in her home, but granting her high social status, she was able to appeal personally to both King Charles II and James II for some level of national religious tolerance, especially for such peace-loving citizens as were the Quakers. Both in and out of prison, for fifty years she penned a significant collection of personal letters, public epistles, and religious pamphlets presenting Quaker theology and ideals. She died at her home at Swarthmoor Hall on April 23, 1702.

A recent historical study of all of Fell's corpus argues persuasively that she was an impressive independent Christian theologian who believed that a person's inner light, affirmed by Quakers as the primary spiritual reality, was the manifestation of a Christ-centered realized eschatology.[1] Responding to the social chaos of her time, she adopted the apocalyptic imagery of especially the book of Revelation to announce that the end time, with Christ's triumphant return, was imminent; that the state church, and laws enforcing it, were evidence of the evils that John's visions had foretold; that the light of the Spirit of Christ was found in the self, not in the erroneous religious accretions maintained by the dominant Christian denominations; and that the voice of the Spirit of the risen Christ always spoke the gospel of peace. This second coming of Christ, already experienced in one's self, replaced all old Christian symbols and rituals, which, similar to those in Judaism, were precursors of the end. She was steeped in the Bible—as was the expectation for all Quakers in the Society's early decades—and was herself a trinitarian Christian, writing of the Light as the triune Godhead of Father, Son, and Spirit.[2] Presenting herself as a millennialist prophet through whom God spoke, she described Jesus as a man of action and the model for her life of religious and political activism.

Her presentation of and her living out the spiritual equality of women and men were remarkable. Although Fell lived after the impressive career of Queen Elizabeth I, who was a highly educated woman fully functioning as authoritative within a man's world, social strictures supporting the subordination of women remained strong in the seventeenth century. Indeed, the Protestant encouragement for personal Bible study in some ways intensified male dominance in church and society by urging women's study of especially those biblical passages that served the patriarchal worldview. However, in 1671, anticipating the ideal of "separate but equal," perhaps inspired by centuries of Roman Catholic women's monastic communities that in some ways skirted male authority, Fell was instrumental in establishing separate women's meetings as the ideal venue for developing and encouraging the religious voices of women, who were recognized as having received, no less than men, the divine inner light.

It was Fell's extensive biblical exegesis in her essay of 1666, *Women's Speaking Justified, Proved and Allowed of by the Scriptures*, written while imprisoned, that for about two centuries led the pursuit of women's equality with men in Christ.[3] Fell's faithfulness as a Christian and her absolute reverence for the Bible are evident in her presentation of both classic and creative hermeneutical arguments, as she addressed the positive as well as the negative biblical passages relating to the spiritual role of women. (So it is that her work contrasts starkly with the tone of ridicule and the rejection of biblical authority that characterize the often-anthologized essays in Elizabeth Cady Stanton's 1895 *The Woman's Bible*.) Fell saw her task as probing the original intent of the Scriptures, and I see her leading the Easter procession, holding high the torch of the light, welcoming women and men to walk together toward the exercise of justice.

She began her essay with an exposition of Genesis 1, asserting that the *imago dei* was granted to both men and women. Relying on the King James Bible translation, she interpreted the story of Genesis 3 as promising that the "seed" of the woman, which was to fight against evil, was not solely Christ, but was all those children of Eve—that is, both women and men—in whom the light of Christ dwelt. She delineated numerous biblical passages in which the people of God were described with female imagery. She discussed Jesus' many interactions with women, as well as the role of women after his resurrection and in the church described in Acts. Her thorough essay concluded with a long apocalyptic exposition of the end time foretold in Revelation as being the current moment, during which both women and men could receive the outpouring of the Spirit and would together bring in the new age. Most noteworthy for a nonacademic theologian was her thoughtful hermeneutical discussion of the contradictory passages in Paul, in which she faced squarely those verses that were used to sideline women in the church, about which she argued that the women whom Paul ordered to keep silent in Corinth were those who had not yet received the Spirit. Thus she claimed that even the epistles affirmed the spiritual—albeit not the social—equality of women with men.

Here's to you, Margaret Fell.

Now to Sunday, and women.

(We might begin with a moment of thanks to God for centuries of Christian sectarians, those religious folk who emphasized one tiny aspect of the faith so obsessively that they skewed everything else. Their single-minded focus—the Quakers refusing participation in war, the Amish resisting consumer values, the Jehovah's Witnesses evangelizing the neighborhood, the snake-handlers relying on divine protection—does hold before our collective face something we too easily can lay aside, and for this we can be grateful.)

The twentieth century witnessed the practice of separate laywomen's worship gatherings among Christians other than Quakers. Certainly for some women, worship apart from oppressive or even abusive male leadership was God's good news, for, as Fell maintained, some women could and would speak more freely—indeed, breathe more easily—when men were out of the room. It's a movement in which I never took part: my feminist contributions to church life, which have been supported and promoted for the most part by egalitarian men holding positions of ecclesial authority, have focused on the texts employed by the full assembly on Sunday morning. Of course, I too have memories of unfortunate episodes with men; but then, given that activists in a movement often criticize colleagues who seem to be out of step, I also had unpleasant interactions with women. When I have not been welcomed, it was I think not my gender that was the issue, but my passion for specific worship reforms. It is, indeed, by no means accurate to assume that women will support causes promoted by other women.

However, in many Protestant churches now, women exercise significant leadership, serving as bishops, heading the ministry in even large parishes, producing worship materials for churchwide use, composing hymns, teaching theology in universities, staffing seminaries, preparing exegetical resources, publishing model sermons. (I hope that sociologists are not correct when suggesting that women are welcomed into positions only after the culture has devalued those tasks.) One might argue that women have finally arrived, that after four hundred years Margaret Fell is vindicated, that women's voices have indeed been heard, that at least in some places in some countries, a Christian woman can join with a worshiping assembly in which she is fully welcomed. Yet is this claim unrealistically optimistic? (What about in one-church-town, red state?) How can a local assembly welcome women, even if the polity of its church body constricts women's roles? And how can women know themselves to be welcomed by Christ, despite their experience of being silenced or even sexually abused by the body of that Christ? Fell sought to justify and indeed to encourage the voices of women in praise, petition, and moral imperative: alas, we aren't there yet.

The anthropology taught during the Middle Ages proposed that God had allotted to males and females the four human qualities—intellect, will, memory, and imagination—in a hierarchical order. Intellect was the highest characteristic and closest to God, and men had more of it than did women, and imagination was the lowest, because it was uncontrollable, and women had more of this than did men. (I was sorry to discover that most of my university students accepted this medieval understanding of gender distinction as being more or less accurate.) This worldview led in the nineteenth century to the assumption that religious sensibilities, which utilized more imagination than intellect (!), were best nurtured by women. So, although Martin Luther had written that the man of the house was to lead family prayers, three centuries later during the Cult of True Womanhood, bringing the children to church and saying prayers at bedtime was up to the mother. Continuing into the twentieth century, the essentialist position argues that in some ways females are by essence, by unavoidable nature, different from males and that one result of this gendered difference renders females more qualified than males to deal with matters religious. (I can't keep all this straight: what are women good at?)

But walk with me out of the twentieth century into the twenty-first, when the simplicity of categorizing humans as either male or female is pretty much over in the Western world. Our welcome on Sunday must be extended to more than women. First came the categories of lesbian, gay, bisexual, and transgender. Now, here are some of the many more terms that begin to describe human sexuality and societal gendering: affirmed gender, agender, asexual, assigned gender, cisgender, gender binary, gender dysphoria, gender expression, gender fluid, gender identity, gender marker, gender neutral, gender nonconforming, genderqueer, intersex, pansexual, sexual orientation, transsexual, third gender. I note in obituaries in the local newspaper that some conservative Christians are using the verb "transitioned" to mean "died and went to heaven," but given our society's evolving vocabulary, other Christians use the term "transitioning" to mean "the process one goes through to discover and/or affirm their gender identity."[4] (Note the grammatical problems English now has: "one" matched with "their.") That transitioning can have two such vastly different meanings would be comic, if it weren't instead a painful sign of two worldviews contending for Christian dominance.

We hear Fell reminding us that the inner light of the Spirit of Christ is manifest in the self, and we are coming to recognize the immense complexity in this self. The mystery of the human person is not surprising if we continue to affirm from Genesis 1:27 that we are in some unknown way made in the image of God, and that of a God who is beyond our easy imaginings. However, some Christians are more intent on affirming, also from Genesis 1:27, that God created two sexes, each with its own gendered destiny—see Genesis 3:16-18—and that citing these passages ought to conclude the inquiry. The issues determined by our interpretations of the narratives in Genesis are multiform. Remember that until the mid-nineteenth century, most Christian authorities forbade dispensing painkillers during childbirth, citing the curse of Eve in Genesis 3:16 as indicating God's intention that every woman suffer with pain during labor.

I suggest that the theological affirmation that we Christians connect ourselves in some mysterious way to the God we worship—humans made in the *imago dei*—has more future than has the detailed description of the created earth in Genesis 1, with its reservoir of rain stored above the sky, with plants given to humankind for food, and, yes, with humans in only two genders. An openness to the human mystery allows for more mercy toward one another, more support for those with whom we walk the way of baptism. Wouldn't it be stunning, in itself a powerful proclamation of the gospel, if all those persons struggling with and against their birth sex and their formative gender were to be welcomed with open arms in the Sunday assembly? (Can transgendered persons serve as greeters or lectors in your assembly?) Can we thank God for inspiring not only historical theologians, but also scientists, psychologists, therapists, and political activists, for their deepening knowledge of the human species? We need to run as fast as we can to stay up with them, so that we can hear their proposals and use their new words to welcome all God's children.

In an epistle to Friends in 1654, Margaret Fell wrote, "To all my Dear Brethren and Sisters who are in the Light, which Christ Jesus hath enlightened you withal, I warn you and

Charge you from the Lord God, that you be faithful and obedient unto the measure of Grace which he hath given to every one of you to profit withal, and that the Light of Christ Jesus in every one of you, lead you and guide you."[5] Note: the Light is given to every one of you. Every Sunday Margaret Fell calls to us to welcome men, women, indeed, everyone. We aren't there yet.

Chapter 8

Assessing Emotion
with Julian of Norwich

A woman whom we know as Julian was born probably in 1342, resided near Norwich, England, and nearly died of an ailment in 1373. While in extremis on a day in May she experienced a series of visions, after which she wrote a short record of the visions, now titled "A Vision Showed to a Devout Woman." At some point she became an anchorite and lived for the remainder of her life in a room affixed to the outside wall of St. Julian's church, which was located in a busy commercial area of Norwich, one of England's largest cities, and from which it seems she took her name. Her tiny dwelling would have had three windows: one to the church, for her continuous attention to the parish liturgies; one to a room for her servant, who had access to the city; and one to the outside world, through which, although probably hidden behind a black curtain,[1] she offered spiritual counseling to visitors. Several fifteenth-century wills include bequests for her maintenance. She contemplated her original and several other visions for over twenty years, and by about 1400 had completed *A Revelation of Love*, a much expanded theological exposition of the meanings of her visions, and the first work extant penned by a woman in the English language.[2] She died sometime after 1416 and was virtually ignored until the mid-twentieth century, when her use of female imagery for God garnered enthusiastic support. The manuscript evidence is

49

unclear: Did her original visions occur on May viii or May xiii? My denomination commemorates her on May 8.

Europe during the eleventh through the fifteenth centuries nurtured an impressive number of visionaries recording their experiences. Some were monastics who spoke of Mother Christ as an inspiration for their own mothering abbot.[3] But Julian's *A Revelation of Love* is judged unique for its spiritual depth and creativity, the novum of "a speculative vernacular theology."[4] She interpreted her visions, not as personal communications from God nor as messages to a monastic community, but rather as comprehensive demonstrations of trinitarian doctrine, a soteriology for the whole church based on God's "one-ing" with us. For Julian, Christ, our Mother, was Wisdom,[5] and since in the Middle Ages wisdom was seen as a masculine trait, she was able to describe Christ with both the female attributes of natural motherhood and the stereotypically male characteristic of wisdom.[6] Julian presents surprising metaphors: I like that Christ was hung up to dry, like wet clothes,[7] and that we are Christ's crown.[8]

One day, perhaps in 1413, she had a visitor named Margery Kempe.

We learn about the illiterate Margery thanks to her having dictated her memoirs to several different assistants.[9] Born probably in 1373 into a prosperous middle-class and politically active family in Lynn, England, Margery tells of her marriage, a bout of postpartum depression, a total of fourteen childbirths, and her workload as a businesswoman. Eventually, after experiencing a vision of Christ, she made an agreement with her husband, solemnized by a priest, to live as a celibate, the idea being that mystically married to Christ, she could no longer function as her husband's sexual partner.[10] In previous centuries, a good number of visionaries had spoken of intimate love with Christ, but Margery's conversations with her beloved Christ are marked by graphic realism: "Therefore you can boldly take me in the arms of your soul and kiss my mouth, my head, and my feet as sweetly as you want," says Jesus to her.[11] Jesus presents her with a wedding ring, in which she is to inscribe the words *Jesus est amor meus*.[12] With no attention to chronology, her memoirs narrate her religious adventures while on pilgrimage to Canterbury, Venice, the Holy Land, Assisi, Rome, Santiago de Compostela, and Aachen. She died sometime after 1439. Although forgotten for nearly five centuries, in 1934 her memoirs were discovered in a private library of some British Roman Catholics, and her remarkable adventures as a medieval woman shaping her own destiny became a source of fascination for contemporary feminists.

During her travels it was her wild emotional outbursts that attracted both the admiration and the scorn of other worshipers and finally even the accusation of heresy by peeved clergy. Repeatedly in her memoirs, which are cast in the third person, "this creature" is described as experiencing uncontrolled fits of sobbings, whenever she heard of the sufferings of Christ or saw a graphic depiction of the crucifixion.[13] Hers was the medieval "gift of tears" gone over the top. For example, during one Holy Week, "she had so much sweetness and devotion that she could not bear it, but cried, wept, and sobbed very violently. She could not resist weeping and sobbing, but she simply had to weep, cry and sob, when she saw her Saviour suffer such great pains for her love."[14] When an archbishop ordered her to calm down, she responded, "Sir, you shall wish some day that you had wept as sorely as I."[15] She took comfort in Jesus saying to her, "Your tears are truly to the angels like spiced and honeyed wine."[16]

On one of her pilgrimages, Margery consulted Julian of Norwich, and her memoirs capture with impressive accuracy the voice of the older visionary: "The Holy Ghost is all charity. . . . The soul of a righteous man is the seat of God."[17] So let us compare Julian, who wrote of Christ as our mother, and Margery, who spoke of Jesus as her husband.

Of family members, Julian mentions only her mother. Margery was married, eventually caring for her incontinent husband, and she bore fourteen children, one of whom she discusses. Julian was an enclosed solitary; the pilgrim Margery traveled across Europe. Julian says nothing about any gainful employment; Margery recalls her obligations in business. The educated Julian penned her own theological work; the illiterate Margery required an amanuensis for her scattered memoirs. Julian focused on the Trinity, Margery on the crucifixion. Julian saw her own sufferings as connecting her to Christ; Margery articulated only the immense distance between her sinful self and the dying Christ. Julian believed that in the eschaton all would be well; Margery presents no such confidence in a future from God. Julian considered sin to be a small thing in the mind of God, while Margery repeatedly sought absolution for her grievous sins. Julian never speaks ill of the clergy; Margery publicly criticized priests for their lax ministries and their disdain of her devotion. Julian's work is permeated with joy, the bliss she finds in God. Margery maintained nearly perpetual lamentation when contemplating the cross.

It is no wonder that, having studied Julian and Margery, I am wary of gender-specific analyses of spirituality.

Of the many ways we might contrast these women when considering our Sunday gatherings, here is one: Julian was an introvert, Margery an extrovert. Both introverts and extroverts are willing and valuable members of groups and civilization at large. But introverts, with their intense inner life, require lots of quiet time, since they find interpersonal connections exhausting, while extroverts are exhilarated by high stimulation, excelling at networking and thriving on interpersonal connections of all kinds. Both such persons are with us today. (Full disclosure: I am more Julian than Margery.)

The church I attended as a child was perfect for introverts. Worship was understood to be a serious undertaking that unites an assembly in contemplative attention to the things of God. No converse between the worshipers was expected. Robust hymn-singing, which is a communal activity with no individualized role, provided the primary outlet for voices. The preacher spoke from the pulpit, his distance granting considerable space to the hearers. My pastors did not tell jokes, so we were not expected to laugh. Pews, which are a godsend to parents of children under the age of six (perched in individual seats, small children cannot take a nap with their head on papa's lap, and their Cheerios fall through onto the floor), restricted everyone by keeping them in line, like words on a page. Such worship reminds me of what Flannery O'Connor wrote about her attendance at daily Mass in one parish during the 1950s: "I went there three years and never knew a soul in that congregation or any of the priests, but it was not necessary. As soon as I went in the door I was at home."[18] In summary, an individual's emotion, which was beside the point of the assembly's faith and liturgy, was best left out in the narthex along with one's wet umbrella.

Fifty years later, the worship of many churches is better designed for extroverts. There is the presumption that the worship is an enjoyable event that forms a community of enthusiastic participants. Upon entering, one is expected to shake hands with a greeter. The worship space may be arranged to maximize interpersonal contact. Some clergy walk up and down the aisle as they preach, relying on an in-your-face method of holding parishioners' attention, and laughter is frequent. Worshipers may call out personal petitions to the intercessions, and they participate in a lengthy and energetic sharing of the peace. The assembly is invited to hold hands, even with strangers, during the Lord's Prayer. The musical accompaniment may be a high-decibel band, and applause—whether meant to include the worshipers in the music or to praise the performers—is commonplace. Conversation in the lounge with sugar snacks that follows worship is so prized that an anthropologist might judge the liturgy's four-fold *ordo* to be gathering, word, meal, and coffee hour.

Charismatic and Pentecostal worship heightens emotional involvement. Although the black Baptist preacher I knew in Philadelphia always maintained that there is "no celebration without education," his magnificent talent at concluding his sermon with whooping did lead the assembly, who by then had been assembled for about two hours, into ecstatic shouts and joyous expressions of glossolalia. At True Bible Way in Natchez, Mississippi, worshipers are encouraged to succumb to the Spirit, "to get the blessing." After the service, a woman who had been slain in the Spirit described the sensation in this way: "It's the most beautiful, beautiful feeling that you can ever experience; it's just past finding out. It makes my heart to rejoice."[19] In such assemblies, emotions are prized as a gift from God unique to each individual, without the expression of which the person is diminished, and successful worship enlivens individual emotion and encourages emotional expression.

Recent studies of introverts and extroverts provide useful material for those of us interested in considering the emotional content of worship.[20] There is considerable evidence that American culture, seen for example in the elementary school system, is unsympathetic to introverts, despite their irrefutable contributions to society, and I am left wondering to what degree the current tendencies toward extroverted worship have less to do with profound theological reflection on Christian ritual and more to do with assemblies simply being American. In our time the multiplicity of denominations allows for at least Americans to choose on Sunday morning between unaccompanied chant and a jazz band, between formal preaching and circles of conversation, between silence and applause, such that introverts may find an assembly that honors their tendencies.

Yet if we merely assume that the church down the block will provide what we do not, we are forgetting that Julian and Margery were co-religionists of the same ethnicity during the same decades, shaped by the same lectionary and the identical liturgy. How can we serve both Julian and Margery, honoring the mystery of each human person, with neither personality disposition judged to be more suitable for the baptized life? Many parishes offer options at different services—the sheep at nine, the goats at eleven, the charismatics at one. Is this the way forward? Or might we construct Sunday worship so that at the same liturgy, the whole people gather, the introverts having space to ponder the proclaimed words and the extroverts having occasion to celebrate together?

   In her conclusion Julian wrote, "For charity's sake, let us pray all together with God's working, thanking, trusting, enjoying. For it is thus that our good Lord willeth us to pray, in the sweet words that he said full merrily 'I am ground of thy beseeching.' "[21] And in his conclusion Margery's recorder wrote, "Ever blessed may God be, for he made her always more mighty and more strong in his love and in his fear, and gave her increase of virtue, with perseverance."[22] So I wish for all of us, thanks to Sunday morning.

Chapter 9

Worshiping in Translation
with Catherine Winkworth

Born in 1827, Catherine Winkworth resided for much of her life in Manchester and then in Clifton, England. The daughter of a silk merchant, she was privately educated and as an adult volunteered in various ways to promote women's rights and girls' education. She lived for a time in Dresden, Germany, where she became familiar with the substantial German chorale tradition of congregational singing, and subsequently she dedicated her considerable linguistic talents to crafting expert translations of German hymns into English. Over the years she released several collections of her translated hymnody under the title *Lyra Germanica*, the first of which adopts a practice from German Lutherans of assigning one hymn to each Sunday of her church's one-year lectionary as an appointed hymn-of-the-day. In 1869 she published an impressive historical study of a thousand years of German song. She died on July 1, 1878, while visiting near Geneva.

Some of the hymns that she selected for translation had been composed during Europe's Thirty Years' War, and reading through these texts stuns us with the magnitude of the sufferings experienced by seventeenth-century believers. Here are some lines from these hymns: "When shall I find some respite, some relief / From this unsleeping pain, this haunting grief, / Struck by the arrows of thy wrath, Most High";[1] "Earth is the home of tears and woe";[2] for Ascension Day, "Lord, on earth I dwell in pain, / Here in anguish I must lie";[3] for a morning hymn, "Once more from rest I rise again, / To greet a day of toil and pain, / My Heavenly-appointed lot";[4] and the quite startling "Go and dig my grave today!"[5] Expressive of life so filled with misery, it is not surprising that many of Winkworth's translations are no longer sung. In some texts, God is indeed the abusive father, who inflicts unmitigated hardships on the faithful to test their loyal submission; yet if they are duly repentant, they will indeed be rewarded in heaven. (Mercifully, this vindictive spirituality is nearly wholly gone from my church.)

However, some of her 440 translated hymn texts remain popular, even beloved, in our time. The hymnal currently in the pew racks of many Lutheran churches includes eighteen of her translations, although some have been emended, and her most masterful texts are ecumenically treasured around the world. Among her most revered hymns are such classics as "Praise to the Lord, the Almighty," "Now Thank We All Our God," "In Thee Is Gladness," "Jesus, Priceless Treasure," "Dearest Jesus, We Are Here," "O Living Bread from Heaven," and the Advent hymn "Comfort, Comfort Now My People." Yet even her joyous hymns are not characterized by a mindless happiness. The stark reality of human suffering is never far away: the second stanza of "Jesus, Priceless Treasure" speaks of molesting foes, a shaking earth, quaking hearts, lightnings and thunders, with sin and death assailing us.[6]

As a translator of texts for Christian worship, Winkworth joins an honored crowd of witnesses, for since its origins, Christianity has been a translation religion, which not all religions are. No neophyte is taught Koine Greek—or perhaps Aramaic?—at baptism. At our very beginning, Paul, writing in Greek to Gentile and Jewish Christians in Romans 8:15, quotes and then translates the Aramaic *Abba* as the Greek *pater*, and like Paul, over the centuries Christians have worked to translate a received tradition so that worship can be conducted in the vernacular. Most missionary efforts in recent centuries have judged it absolutely necessary to catechize and worship in the people's speech. It is as if a God who chooses incarnation naturally prefers to communicate with the people in their own language. Indeed, over the centuries Christian missionaries had to design alphabets and formulate written syntax so they could translate the Scriptures into languages that had been solely oral. By the way, these missionary efforts sometimes now encounter condemnation for having reduced so many of the world's languages to writing (although I find it odd that we call this task "reducing").

However, translation can never be absolutely accurate. Although the Christian tradition baptized the title "Father," *Abba* seems to be closer to "Papa," which is not a term with which English-speaking Christians address God on Sunday morning. For centuries, Christian translators have described both the necessity and the difficulty of their work. Jerome explained that such work cannot be word for word: "The result will sound uncouth. . . . I have always aimed at rendering sense, not words."[7] Martin Luther defended his biblical translation thus: "We do not have to inquire of the literal Latin, how we are to speak German, as these asses do. (!!) Rather we must inquire about how to speak German of the mother in the home, the children on the street, the common man in the market-place."[8] In the 1950s, the committee that produced the Revised Standard Version described its task this way: "The best that can be hoped is an approximation to the thought of the original, but its finer points, its overtones, its allusions, the feeling and atmosphere of its words lie beyond any process of translation."[9] So, "Father" is something, but not everything, of *Abba*, and it brings its own connotations into our prayer—which some worshipers find gratifying, others not so much.

Yet this approximation in sacred vocabulary is all that we have, despite the focus in our religion on the preeminence of the word of God—a somewhat unsettling realization. This linguistic understanding leads us to assert that any textual fundamentalism is wrongheaded, that all enshrinement of historic liturgical resources misjudges the reality of language.

Yet I know that the debate is by no means resolved. Many groups of Christians—some entire denominations—defend a translation that for some reason is most sacred to them, and the resulting quarrels over whether a new translation is warranted and whether it ought to adhere to formal correspondence or to rely on dynamic equivalence have brought much sorrow to Christian communities.[10]

In 1978 while studying at Union Theological Seminary, I submitted a master's thesis entitled "Lutheran Liturgical Prayer and God as Mother,"[11] and for that project I traced the history of Christian use of the title "Father" for God. Since then, like riding on a roller coaster, I have joined with one committee and retreat seminar after another to discuss whether "Father" is the Christian God's privileged first name, or its doctrinally mandated formulation, or a biblically required title, or a beloved metaphor, or a patriarchal remnant that sanctifies discrimination against women. In medieval Europe, God was mostly King, but in the nineteenth century, with kings fading away, God became overwhelmingly Father. Depending on the church, Father remains dominant or shares its dais with other biblical and theological titles and metaphors, and newly composed hymns offer the worshiping assembly a multiform God to adore. (Is the usage in your denomination of "Father" what you judge it ought to be?) Is the title "Father" newly acceptable, given the widespread dismissal of the women's movement? Is the title still honored, but with diminished authority? It seems that some believers in old age reclaim the worldview of their childhood, elderly theologians making peace with their Father.[12] Is this metaphor still widely misunderstood—as if our God is none other than Zeus having impregnated some virgin to sire our Hercules?

By the way, in several of her hymns, Winkworth translated the German term *Vaterherz* as "Father-heart," which I like immensely.[13] I am sorry this has been discarded along the way.

We encounter three of the most common designations for God in the opening line of what is perhaps Winkworth's most well-known hymn. The line "Praise to the Lord, the Almighty, the King of creation" begins her translation of Joachim Neander's 1680 German *Lobe den Herren, den mächtigen König der Ehren*. In rendering the German *Herr*, Winkworth used the English term Lord, that double-sided word that contains both the Hebrew tetragrammaton of God's name YHWH and the Greek title of respect for the master Jesus. In another hymn, she names each person of the Trinity as Lord: "The Lord, the Maker, with us dwell. . . . The Lord, the Saviour, Light Divine. . . . The Lord, the Comforter, be near."[14] As with "Father," some traditional uses of "Lord" are now being replaced with alternatives, some more theologically profound than others. As an American, in a culture with no functioning lords (outside of the entertainment provided by British television series), I am glad that Winkworth rendered the original *Herr* with Lord, rather than with some version of mere Mister. Indeed, I find it difficult to sing Spanish hymns, filled as they are with *Señor*, and I am grateful to the innovative translator who rendered the *Señor* in Cesáreo Gabaráin's contemporary Spanish hymn with the two-dimensional "Sweet Lord."[15]

Next, Winkworth rendered the German adjective *mächtigen* (powerful) with one of the most common descriptors for God: "the Almighty." The Septuagint, in translating Genesis 17:1, just gave up trying to translate the divine name *El Shaddai*, presenting it only as "your God." However, the Vulgate cast this *El Shaddai* as *Deus omnipotens*, and most Christian tradition has continued the custom of translating the ambiguous Hebrew as "Almighty God." Is the adjective "almighty" a worthy rendering of *shaddai*, which recalls either the twin mountain peaks on the horizon of pre-Israelite Canaanites or the twin breasts (*shad* = breast) of the great goddess?[16] Here Christian speech has replaced an image from nature with a benign adjective. The same has occurred in our time, when *Sabaoth*, those heavenly armies of angels, is rendered "power and might." Has this practice of substitution exalted or demoted God?

Winkworth's verbal choices in addressing God include strong metaphors. There is her use of "king" in this hymn, although in surprisingly few others. What should American

Christians do with this metaphor? One of Winkworth's Advent hymns calls Jesus "the true Joshua" who will bring the people into their promised land.[17] Would contemporary worshipers understand this use of "Joshua"? Her hymn for St. Stephen's Day calls Christ "the Gideon who shall rise to save us."[18] Do our assemblies know who Gideon was? In an Easter hymn the rocky cave of Christ's tomb is contrasted with "Thyself the Rock of our Salvation."[19] She introduced into the text of the German hymn *In dir ist Freude* the metaphor "Jesus, Sunshine of my heart."[20] In a nature hymn that praises the earth's waters, she calls God "the Fountain whence all gladness flows,"[21] and one hymn includes the line "Graft me into Thee for ever, Tree of Life, that I may grow."[22] At least these several metaphors would find resonance among us.

Some recent hymnals include "Many and Great, O God," a text affectionately called the Dakota Hymn, Philip Frazier's 1929 translation of Joseph R. Renville's 1842 poem.[23] In the original Dakota language, the opening words addressed *Wakantanka*. Was it appropriate for nineteenth-century Christians to begin use of this Lakota title as the name of God? Among the traditional Lakota, *Wakantanka* names the sixteen-fold mystery of the earth, its four cycles of the seasons, four phases of the moon, four times of the day, and four of the night.[24] *Wakantanka* is not personified, not a single being, but rather those great supernatural powers that the petitioner invokes. "*Wakantanka* could never have a son."[25] What do those current Native peoples who retain their traditional beliefs think of this adaptation of their practice? Does that matter to us?

Some Christians defend the practice of referring to the church as a she. This grammatical usage arose when the languages spoken by Christians were gendered speech, and— probably unconsciously—echoed ancient imagery of the divine intercourse between the male deity and his female consort. In American English, gendered speech has dropped out of use, although some sailors still speak of their ship as a she—the men enjoying their ride on top of the supine vessel that carries them in joy to distant places. But in my speech, a ship and a nation and the church are all "it." In my church's worship book, the entire Psalter and many hymns have eliminated divine masculine pronouns, and I am relieved at this removal of stumbling blocks. I realize that after several millennia of divine masculine terminology, women are rather accustomed to it, and surely some worshipers are glad of a benign he in their lives. The pronoun question must be continually asked of theologians, translators, and preachers, and I hope there will come a time when the majority of Christians will reject the portrayal of God as a Great Big He in the sky. However, Winkworth's "Praise to the Lord, the Almighty" includes eleven uses of the male pronoun, thus prompting one current hymnal to print also an inclusive emending of her text, in which God is not "he" but "you."[26]

In her translation of "Easter Song," Winkworth praises God for the springtime, during which even the birds sing their adoration—a commonplace in nineteenth-century hymns and poems—but not my favorite way to speak of Christ's resurrection. (Did Winkworth know that birds sing to mark their territory?) But the same hymn includes a remarkable tribute to other speech than that of her English Protestants:

> Thou art the Pascha to the Greek,
> And still we hear the Jew
> Of thee as Passover doth speak,
> And Latins know thee too
> As Transitus, that crowns the Holy Week.[27]

Although no longer in use, this surprising text reminds us of the perennial Christian questions about the vocabulary of our worship, translation debates, denominational preferences, and ecumenical sharing. (Should English speakers call Resurrection Day Pascha rather than Easter?)

And, of course, as the conversations proceed, who gets the last word?

Thank you, Catherine Winkworth, for your gifts to us all.

10
Chapter

Comprehending the Readings
with Jerome

Jerome—biblical scholar, textual critic, translator, commentator, biographer, correspondent, polemicist—was the foremost Scripture authority among the church fathers. Called a pioneer in biblical criticism, he was honored by having his name attached to the editions of the massive twentieth-century *Jerome Biblical Commentary*.[1] His voice—learned beyond compare, constitutionally oppositional, ardently defensive, and sometimes excessively nasty—urges us to continue the search for the Christian meaning of biblical texts.

Born in 347 in a small town in northern Italy,[2] he died on September 30 in perhaps 420, having lived in one significant Christian city after another—Rome, Trier, Antioch, Constantinople, Bethlehem—for as a translator and commentator, he sought to know firsthand the specifics of biblical references and geography. He was present at the Council of Constantinople in 381. Recent biographers warn readers against accepting Jerome's own memoirs as an accurate record of his early life, and there is much we cannot know of him: for example, when did he learn Hebrew, and how expert at the language was he? How did he acquire such an extensive and exceedingly costly personal library? Whether living as a hermit, a monk, or a priest, in residence near Rome's papal headquarters or in a Palestinian cave, he dedicated his years to mastering biblical texts, detecting copyist errors, composing commentaries, judging among available translations, and providing much of his own work in translation toward the goal of a Latin—thus vernacular—translation of the Bible from the Hebrew and Greek.

(At a Roman Catholic university in a course titled "The Church and Women," having read the assigned selections by Jerome, a student called out, "This guy had issues." Indeed. Jerome's honoring of women was in direct proportion to their resembling celibate men. But he shared this worldview with most of his contemporaries, albeit his virulence on the topic could be extreme. Yet may we all be honored for our positive contributions to the life of faith, rather than pilloried because of our issues.)

At least since the fourth century, churches have preferred one of two opposite approaches in biblical interpretation: the Antiochian preference for literal meaning and the Alexandrian delight in allegorical significance. These two were combined in Jerome. He wrote, "The words of Scripture are not simple, as some suppose; much is concealed in them. The letter indicates one thing, the mystical language another."[3] He theorized that the literal is always to be applied first, but if the literal accorded no meaning of value, the church was to go further to what Jerome called "the higher interpretation." For example, in commenting on Christ's entry into Jerusalem in Matthew 21, Jerome explains that the literal meaning of Jesus riding on two animals, a donkey and a colt, is nonsensical. However, if the donkey represented Israel, which had been trained in Torah, and the colt represented the Gentiles, who had not yet received the word of God, the meaning of the passage would be that Christ brought salvation to the whole world.[4] It's not our exegetical style, but I commend Jerome for struggling to comprehend the Scriptures.

Although his Vulgate eventually reigned in the Western church for a millennium, it had taken the conservative forces who controlled liturgical decisions several centuries to agree to replace their Old Latin version with his translation. (Ah: when is liturgical conservatism religiously appropriate, and when is it merely obstructionist? I hear a member of the worship committee saying, "But the binding of our old Bible is so beautiful. . . .") The most strenuous opposition Jerome met with was his assertion that when translating the Old Testament, Christians should be working with the Hebrew text of the Tanakh, rather than with the Greek of the Septuagint. A story is told of one reaction to Jerome's translation of the book of Jonah, in which his rendering the plant in chapter 4 as "ivy" rather than the traditional "gourd" led to a vociferous brouhaha by worshipers who condemned him for changing the Bible.[5] Our various Bibles now refer to a bush, a climbing gourd, a castor-oil plant, a vine: which translation gets your vote? Does it matter?

The various biblical translations chosen by our churches for use on Sunday morning demonstrate the ongoing debate about which mind ought to govern the translation of the Old Testament for Christian worship. We can lament that Jerome assumed a copyist error when Romans 16:7 calls Junia an apostle: surely, thought Jerome, with his mind shaped by Greek culture, the original text would have designated only a male, Junius, to be an apostle. But for a more current debate: although the Hebrew noun *almah* in Isaiah 7:14 means merely "young woman," Jerome's belief that the Old Testament led to the New, bolstered by his dedication to the ideal of celibacy, led him to render the Hebrew noun as "virgin," thus coordinating this passage with the Gospels' stories of a virgin birth. (It is illuminating to compare contemporary Bible translations of this text: first, check the denominational home of the translators; second, guess which translations will render the Isaiah passage with "virgin" and which with "young woman"; finally, smile if you guessed correctly.) On the feast of the Annunciation, when proclaiming Isaiah 7:10-14, which is most important: precise translation of the Hebrew, coordination with the Gospel reading of Luke 1, or maintenance of traditional church teaching? How do we choose among these?

For Jerome, and for much of the history of Christian theology, the parts of the Hebrew scriptures that offered the most significance for Christians were the prophets and the psalms. For example, Jerome looks to Psalm 118:25—"Save us, we beseech you, O Lord!"—to explain the meaning of the people's cry "Hosanna" on Palm Sunday, a useful exercise in our own time, when that cry is by many worshipers thought to mean "Three cheers for Jesus!"[6] The contemporary version of Jerome's method is found in the consensus of biblical scholars who note the parallels between the psalms of lament and the passion narratives. Since the Gospel accounts of Christ's suffering and death were composed by first-century believers who were not present at the crucifixion, they relied for the details in their narratives on what they knew: the psalms.

The fact is that the New Testament is a gloss on the Old, and we require the Old when interpreting the New. In the Nicene Creed, we affirm Paul's claim in 1 Corinthians 15:4 that Christ was raised "in accordance with the scriptures," which means of course the Hebrew scriptures. For Jerome, all the essentials of Christian belief—even the resurrection—are hidden in the Old Testament. As Jerome wrote to Pope Damasus, "Whatever we read in the Old Testament, that we find also in the Gospel; and what was gathered together in the Gospel, this is drawn forth from the authority of the Old Testament: nothing is discordant, nothing diverse. In both Testaments the Trinity is made known."[7] In some English-language translations of Genesis 1, God spoke the word of creation as the Spirit of God moved over the water; this rendering expresses the Christian doctrinal belief that it was the Trinity—God, the Word of God, and the Spirit of God—and not only God the Father who created the world. However, in several recent translations, *ruah* has become a wind, since some contemporary biblical translators in choosing among options do not lean toward an explicitly Christian interpretation of the Hebrew text. Can we trust our preachers to make clear the Christian importance of the text, whichever translation is proclaimed?

Over the last half century, perhaps in response to the horror of the Holocaust and the Christian anti-Semitism that had supported it, some Christian voices argue that the church must interpret the Hebrew scriptures only in accord with their original intent. Will we search for this meaning from the wisdom of ancient Israelites, first-century Jews, contemporary Judaism— whether Orthodox, Conservative, Reform, or Reconstructionist—or the Society of Biblical Literature? Which of these can in any way illumine Christian faith? I have appreciated the image of the Scriptures as a massive elm tree with two major branches that developed simultaneously over the centuries: the Hebrew scriptures of the Israelite people serve as the trunk of the tree; one branch grew into the post-biblical texts central to modern Judaism, the Mishnah and the whole of the Talmud; and the other branch produced the New Testament and Christian exegetical writings. "Judaism and Christianity are grounded in two different interpretations of the same tradition."[8] Thinking of the Old Testament as the trunk of the elm tree, without implying that only one of its branches has enduring value and the other a sucker that can be lopped off, our reliance on the Hebrew scriptures need not lead toward a supersessionism that denies God's voice in either an original or a current Jewish interpretation of the text.

Although Jerome stressed the importance of the prophets and the psalms for Christian interpretations, recently some Christians have emphasized the narratives in the Hebrew scripture as more engaging and accessible. Of the preference for highlighting the Old Testament stories, I remind all non-fundamentalists: these are stories. Stories. And I genuinely ask why ought twenty-first-century Christians to care about which of these ancient stories. That in a patriarchal culture, not one of the males that the story line traces—not Seth, Isaac, Jacob, Judah, David, Solomon, not one—was the oldest son: now, that is a pattern that is useful for Christians. But merely because a story is found in the Bible does not ensure its value for the baptized. Think of the unsettling narrative in 2 Samuel 6 in which the unfortunate Uzzah, attempting to steady the ark of the covenant on its cart, was struck dead by God for touching the holy chest: this is not a useful biblical model as we encourage communicants to assist the minister by holding on to the stem of the chalice as they drink. Although Christians should be encouraged to study the whole of the Bible, I suggest that on Sunday morning it is paramount that our selections nurture Christian faith, and for that task, we need to join Jerome in comprehending the Scriptures for the assembled baptized community. Lutherans would say: find the gospel, whether in the Old or the New Testaments, and rejoice in its proclamation.

In many ways, both versions of the three-year ecumenical lectionary—the Roman Lectionary and the Revised Common Lectionary—show their debt to Jerome. Jerome taught that the New Testament required connection with the Old for Christian interpretation, and so in these lectionaries, the first reading usually appoints a passage from the Hebrew scriptures that in some way complements or illumines the gospel reading.[9] Jerome valued the prophetic passages as essential for christological understanding, and so it is that many of our first readings are messianic oracles and poems. He judged that the deuterocanonical books ought not be held with the same reverence as the other Hebrew scriptures, and so at least in the Revised Common Lectionary, any readings appointed from the deuterocanonical books are assigned also a canonical alternate. Jerome urged that the psalms be recognized as providing Christian meaning, and so our lectionaries encourage the weekly chanting of lengthy passages of the Psalter. In order to accommodate both the Christians who seek always for an Old Testament connection to the gospel reading and those who want a more chronological engagement with the Hebrew scriptures, the Revised Common Lectionary provides two options for the Sundays between Trinity and Reign of Christ. On these Sundays, one option appoints passages from the Pentateuch to be read semi-continuously in Year A, the court histories in Year B, and the prophets in Year C, the idea—does everyone get this?—being that these large swaths of the Hebrew scriptures are seen to illumine Matthew, Mark, and Luke, each in their turn. Thus, in this way, even a Calvinist preference in Bible reading attends to Jerome. He modeled the intense and endless intellectual study of the Scriptures, and hearing his call over the centuries, our biblical scholars and religious publishing houses have produced mountains of liturgical commentary to assist the faithful in comprehending the readings of the lectionary and incorporating its words into daily life.

But I hear Jerome's caustic voice still yelling at us. Are we searching for the Christian meaning of the Scriptures (rather than merely the Wide Truths of Life therein)? For the Christian meaning, as Jerome reminds us, much is concealed. On each Thursday, are we emailing our parishioners short descriptions of the three readings that are appointed for the coming Sunday? Are we including some instruction for Christian comprehension of the proclaimed texts in the printed materials we distribute to the assembly? Are there at least definitions of biblical vocabulary? Are we offering Bible classes that coordinate with the lectionary?

In his sermon on Psalm 42 for those readying for baptism at Easter, Jerome said, "Just as those deer yearn for the water fountains, so do our deer who have withdrawn from Egypt and the world and killed the Pharaoh in their deeds, slaying his whole army in baptism; after the slaying of the devil they long for the fountains of the Church, namely the Father, the Son and the Holy Spirit. Since we have been rescued from the waters we have begun to see the sun, we have commenced to look on the true light. With joy we have said to our soul, Hope in God. . . . Let us interpret the profound mysteries of the Scripture by other witnesses of the Scripture. Everything which we cannot discover in the abyss of the Old Testament we will find revealed in the New, in the roar of God's cataracts, that is to say, in his prophets and apostles."[10] With such a gloss can the sometimes incomprehensible biblical speech proclaim the gospel among Christians. Thank you, Jerome, for goading Christians on toward the comprehension of the Scriptures.

Chapter 11

Chanting the Psalms with Benedict

Benedict, the father of Western monasticism, lived from about 480 to 547. He is remembered as having had a twin sister named Scholastica. After a period of education in Rome, he spent three years as a hermit in a cave not far from Rome, an experience which seems to have made him aware of the benefits of community life. His spirituality became a magnet drawing many persons to him, whom he organized into small communities. By 525 he had moved south to Monte Cassino, where he established his primary monastery, from which developed the worldwide Benedictine communities of men and of women. He remained a layman throughout his life. All that survives from his pen is the remarkable Rule that he composed for monastic life, for which he advised a kindly daily balance of more or less eight hours of prayer, eight hours of sleep, and eight hours of agricultural work, charity, and spiritual reading. His Rule avoids all physical austerities, which at the time of the collapse of the Roman Empire were closely associated with the monastic life, as well as all religious nonsense. Rather, he described the monastery as a school for the Lord's service, all its members growing year by year in communal humility and compassion. He died on March 21, but since that date usually falls during Lent, the West commemorates him instead on his traditional birth date, July 11. (Be sure to greet all your Benedictine friends on July 11 with a "Happy Feast Day" email.)

Fifty years after Benedict's death, Pope Gregory, himself a Benedictine, interviewed four of Benedict's monastic colleagues and composed a "Life" of the monk, which narrated dozens of the miracles being attributed to him. Given that the tradition so highly honors Gregory the Great and so profoundly reveres Benedict, many contemporary historians have a difficult time distancing themselves from this hagiographical account. It seems to me that Benedict's timeless wisdom about the gracious maintenance of a community of persons in lifelong vows is miracle enough for us to contemplate and commemorate.

It is chapters 8–19 of Benedict's Rule, the pattern for the weekly chanting of the Psalter, that continues to be a school for Christian living for those of us who live outside of Benedictine communities. This *Opus Dei*, the communal prayer of the 150 psalms, was Benedict's proposal for what constituted the primary work of the monk. That Benedict himself was steeped in the Psalter is evident in that his Rule cites the psalms over sixty times.[1] When in my thirties, I asked a Dominican friar to teach me how to pray, he introduced me to Benedict's discipline by mailing me the four volumes of the Divine Office. For although as a child I would have heard the church choir singing snatches of the psalms as the opening introit of the Sunday's liturgy, I would seldom have prayed the psalms myself. I have an early memory of finding in the version of Psalm 22 printed in my church's hymnal—some psalms being included in the book for use at morning prayer and evening prayer, which, despite the intentions of the worthy hymnal committee, were never scheduled at my congregation—a verse thanking God for having saved me "from the horns of the unicorns": but since even as a child I knew my fairy tales, in which unicorns are wondrous beasts that granted wishes, why would I want to be kept away from them? The current translation is "the horns of wild bulls." Anyway, inadequate translations notwithstanding, we never prayed the psalms. Benedict did.

When people inquire how best to interest worshipers in the multiplicity of biblical images for God, I direct them to the matchless Psalm 18. In this one psalm, God, who is "my strength," is likened to a rock, a fortress, a deliverer, a shield, and "the horn of my salvation"—an image the intention of which eludes even biblical scholars. God is in a heavenly temple, resembles the smoke and fire of a volcano, rides a cherub, descends to earth in thunder and lightning, has nostrils that quiver with rage. God is "my support" and yet functions also as our judge. God is our light, a commander of armies, an instructor of soldiers, to whom I sing praises and who makes me the head of the nations. My favorite parts of Psalm 18 are verse 2, in which God is our fortress, the wall that keeps us safe, and verse 29, in which God helps us to leap over a wall. Which do you need, the protection of a wall or escape over a wall? All this in one psalm.

Thanks to the extraordinary liturgical discernment of those who constructed the Roman Lectionary, also we Protestants, who now treasure our version of this three-year lectionary, participate weekly in praying the Psalter. No longer are these ancient Hebrew poems only excerpted for short processional pieces presented by the choir; now long passages from the psalms are given to us all. Reviving a pattern first recorded by Athanasius,[2] the psalm follows the first reading, which is usually from the Old Testament. We hear the reading and then say, simply and profoundly, "Yes, we too are part of that story,"[3] and we use a Jewish poem to serve as Christian response to the reading. But we have a lot of work to do to assist worshipers in understanding why the assembly is invited to participate in chanting the psalms. Only seldom is "the sacramental power of the psalms in the liturgy"[4] fully realized, and there are several reasons why.

First, many believers understand praying as a predominantly personal intercession, with a few expressions of individualized gratitude thrown in. However, throughout most of the Sunday liturgy, my addressing personal petitions to God is less important than is the assembly's invoking the Spirit to form the gathered motley crew into one baptized people of faith. Hoping to keep up attendance at worship, clergy may be wary about stressing that in the liturgy we pray mostly for us and for them, rather than for me. For Sunday is not primarily about me; rather, through the readings, the font, the bread and wine, the art, the hymns, the preaching, and the prayers, I once again, at the outset of each week, discover myself to be part of the Body of Christ.

Am I depressed? Well, I join the community in praising God. Am I rejoicing in last week's good fortune? Together we lament the sorrows of humanity. The individual is becoming the communal, and we who care about the liturgy proceed in the hope that worship can work to convert the self into community. (Do contemporary people even wish for such a conversion? There's the data that although more individuals than in the past are bowling for pleasure, membership in bowling clubs is way down.)[5] Indeed, even for the Jews of Jesus' day, the collection of poems that became the book of Psalms had evolved from the individual to the communal. "The Lord is my shepherd" is worded in the singular, but it was chanted by the group, the "my" understood as "our." By myself, this week, I may not know God to be my shepherd, but together, in the flock, we practice such faith.

A second issue is my same old song: the psalms are poems comprised of one metaphor after another. Think back to the Jews of Jesus' day: many first-century worshipers were urban dwellers who, like us, may have had virtually no contact with shepherds. The historical situation of a society of nomadic herders had become a mythic memory, a metaphor to gather the people's hearts, if not their minds, into prayer and praise. For those of us whose spirituality is formed by the three-year lectionary, our task in chanting the psalms is twofold: we need not only to appreciate metaphor, but also to be instructed in a christological code of meaning. One commentator speaks of Benedict's monks as obligated to engage in the study of psalm texts, without which their daily prayer would be unable "to bring them to the summit of monastic perfection in the exercise of contemplative love."[6] Have we engaged our assembles in any study of psalm texts? Is a translation pony of Christian

meaning available? At least I still find useful the Christian
interpretation of Psalm 23 taught by the fathers, in which the
green pastures are catechesis, the still waters the font, the table
the Eucharist, the oil chrismation.[7] Of course, this was not the
original intention of Psalm 23. But such application of the poetic imagery gives me Christian reason to chant the ancient
poem on the fourth Sunday of Easter each year.

In some cases, the Christian gloss of the psalm has contrib-
uted substantially to the centuries of the imagination of the
baptized. That the royal Psalm 72 speaks of kings offering gifts
to the Anointed One has led to the Christian legend that the
magi of Matthew 2 were kings. On the Ascension, Christians
chant the words of Psalm 47, "God has gone up with a shout,"
and so affirm Luke's depiction of Jesus being carried up into
heaven. That the evangelists cite poetic descriptions of human
suffering from the lament Psalm 22 has provided Christians
with details of Golgotha that are powerfully formative for
Christian reflection on Christ's passion.

But on the first Sunday of Advent in Year A, as we chant
Psalm 122, I wonder if "the city of Jerusalem" is heard as a
reference to the church or to the reign of God, or whether it
evokes only the contemporary city with its current political
and religious agonies. On the first Sunday of Advent in Year
B, as we chant Psalm 80, is the Christian meaning of the reference to "Israel" clear? And what about "the one at your right
hand" in verse 17? Does everyone know what Christians
means by this ancient phrase? On the first Sunday of Advent
in Year C, Psalm 25 praises God for the covenant. Would worshipers remember what "the covenant" is? How can we provide this glossary of Christian interpretation to our assemblies?
Is the ubiquitous service folder one venue for such education?
Indeed, if the psalms are chanted without meaning, ought they
be chanted at all? How much meaning is enough? What would
Benedict say about this?

Here's another question. Which method serves the assembly's spirituality more fully: for everyone to chant the psalm

passage, perhaps in alternating verses, or for the congregation to listen to the cantor or choir, while providing only the antiphon? Or, indeed, no antiphon at all? Which is better to engage, our mouths or our ears? Or on some Sundays one, on some Sundays the other?

Benedict concludes chapter 19 of his Rule with this sentence: "Let us take part in the psalmody in such a way that our mind may be in harmony with our voice."[8] Note: our mind, our voice, the Body of Christ as one in lament and in praise.

Chapter 12

Preaching the Faith
with Mary Magdalene

I have a childhood memory of finding in my Lutheran church's worship book the propers for July 22, Mary Magdalene's Day. My retrogressive congregation did not observe this commemoration, but that the hymnal listed the biblical texts for her day demonstrated that other Lutherans did. Perhaps my consuming interest in lectionary is rooted in my early discovery that the churchwide-appointed readings offer more Bible than many parishes can handle. A fully ignited lectionary might burn us right up. In honor of Mary Magdalene, let me address history's homiletical approach to this saint and how she might best influence preaching in our time.

In the past, the usual gospel for July 22 was the story from Luke 7:35-50 of the unnamed sinner anointing Jesus' feet—although the more christologically interesting narrative was the story in Mark 14 of the unnamed woman anointing Jesus' head. The assignment of Luke 7 to Mary Magdalene's Day accorded with the biblical interpretation firmly established in 591 when Pope Gregory the Great, preaching at San Clemente in Rome, gave his stamp of approval to the tradition that the unnamed sinner, carrying her alabaster jar of ointment, was none other than Mary Magdalene, who later carried her jar of myrrh to the tomb. Perhaps such patristic harmonizing meant mostly to simplify the Scriptures, to ease catechesis for pre-literate believers. (In which contexts is this children's Bible approach commendable?) Perhaps these preachers appreciated the symmetry of holding the two jars next to each other. (In your place of worship, does the artistic depiction of Magdalene include her jar? Does it mean to evoke the sinner of Luke 7, the disciple of John 20, or both?) Centuries of Western artists painting the crucifixion have relished the contrast between a gorgeous whore and a faithful believer.[1] The penitent prostitute depicted with bare shoulders and mounds of disheveled red curly hair balances the heavily shrouded Mother Mary, the antithetical women flanking the cross and each typifying half of womanhood in churches the world over. (Alas, even I, thirty years ago in an early publication, played with the differences between Mary Magdalene and Mary, the mother of our Lord. In a subsequent edition, I overhauled that passage.)[2]

Gregory's sermon in 591 was only the most influential of countless homiletical treatments of Mary Magdalene. Other legends of Magdalene, both alive and dead, the woman sinner, penitent, and contemplative, proliferate.[3] A homily preached by the Anglo-Saxon Aelfric reported about the wedding of Cana, at which Mary Magdalene was to marry John the Evangelist, but John's astonishment at the miracle of the water become wine compelled him to a life of celibacy. (What ought be contemporary Christian sexual ethics?) A prize-wining saga was popularized by the eleventh-century monks of Vézelay and their entrepreneurial Abbot Geoffrey about the progress of Mary Magdalene's bones here and there. (How are pilgrimages to faux relics religiously beneficial?) Since legends stay alive by accumulating layers, the biblical Marys were not enough, and later preachers and artists blended Mary Magdalene with Mary of Egypt. (Always, women's hair. For an astonishing depiction of Magdalene's hair, go online to check out Eric Gill's 1922 crucifix.)[4]

A tour-de-force on Magdalene is the twelfth-century anonymous Cistercian novella entitled *The Life of Saint Mary Magdalene and of Her Sister Saint Martha*.[5] Presented as biography, in parts stunningly sensual, the work cleverly elaborates on the

New Testament—Magdalene's seven demons having been replaced with the seven gifts of the Spirit. She is identified with both Magdala and Bethany because her wealthy family owned property in both places. The reason Martha of Bethany requests Mary's help in serving the meal is that all Jesus' twelve apostles and seventy-two of his disciples are guests for dinner. Yet about some legends, the author writes, "But the rest of the tale—that after the ascension of the Saviour, she immediately fled to the Arabian desert; that she remained there without any clothing in a cave . . . is false and a fabrication of story-tellers."[6] (How to winnow the grain from the chaff remains the task of those who honor the saints.)[7]

Eight centuries before the three-year ecumenical lectionary, the remarkable Cistercian author refused to conflate the New Testament accounts of the resurrection: "That I might not wander even a little from the sense of the evangelists, I have taken care to relate each of their accounts. This seems a better course than others have followed."[8] When Magdalene sees the risen Christ in the garden, the author writes, "The grain of mustard, which Jesus the good gardener had sown in the garden of her heart, took root there, growing into a great tree, most steadfast in faith."[9] After the ascension, Magdalene used her precious ointments for "his living body . . . for the necessities of the disciples."[10] Before turning to tales of Martha, the author concludes, "Among the daughters of men, only the Queen of Heaven is equal to and greater than Mary Magdalene."[11] I find fascinating the combination of this author's dedication to critical biblical studies and credulity concerning saints' legends.

Biblical interpretation has moved along, followed by lectionary reform. As with the Orthodox, who never signed on to Western conflation of Luke 7 with John 20, Mary Magdalene is now being honored as "apostle to the apostles." The Western lectionaries now appoint John 20:11-18 for July 22, Mary Magdalene as the first witness to the resurrection, commissioned as preacher by the risen Christ to announce to the men, "I have seen the Lord." As the newly composed stanza to the hymn "By All Your Saints" has it,

> For Magdalene we praise you, steadfast at cross and tomb.
> Your "Mary!" in the garden dispelled her tears and gloom.
> Apostle to the apostles, she ran to spread the word;
> send us to shout the good news that we have seen the Lord.[12]

On Sundays in our lectionaries, Magdalene appears in the long form of the passion in Years A and B and annually on Easter, always and only faithful to Christ crucified and risen.

Also, on the Sunday when Luke 7:36-50 is appointed (could somebody please standardize our churches' various titles of Sundays?), the gospel now includes the verses that follow, Luke 8:1-3, in which Mary Magdalene, "from whom seven demons had gone out," is named as one of Jesus' traveling entourage and perhaps also as one of those who bankrolled the movement. The first reading for that Sunday narrates Nathan's accusation of David. Thus, next to the unnamed woman standing at the feet of the Savior is the King of Israel sitting on his throne, both inviting us to confession. The second reading, in happy coincidence, finds us reading through Galatians 2, justified by grace and living by faith. The lectionary thus offers to the preacher plenty of ingredients to cook with, without spicing up the menu with tasty bits from Magdalene's love life.

Despite the scholarly industry of probing the second to fourth centuries' gnostic gospels for their spins on Magdalene, at least during the Sunday liturgy the canonical Scriptures are what we have. Yet imaginative embellishment of the lean biblical references is popular in contemporary preaching. Some Christian preachers are now employing the techniques of midrash—the Jewish pattern of storytelling in which the Scripture's narrative gaps are filled up with imagined details. In such midrashic practice, the preachers rummage through their own imagination, so as to suggest what King David was thinking and what the Jesus of this Sunday's Gospel was feeling.

We hear about the emotions of Eve, albeit that she never existed. In my assemblies of choice, this practice of shuffling together the scriptural record and the preacher's imagination is rare. I question whether such narrative accretions—what at the cross and then at the tomb Magdalene was saying, or thinking, or even wearing—are as creative as they strive to be. Such embellishments say far more about the preacher's formation and preferences (do also you dread the sermon on Super Bowl Sunday?) than about either the Bible or the Christian faith, and I question the claim of one homiletician that "people to whom you preach want to know who you are."[13] (Am I supposed to be interested, week after week, year after year, in my pastor's autobiography?)

The current enthusiasm for biblical narrative has developed into a vogue for "narrative preaching," a practice that encourages preachers to invent one detail after another, to flesh out the biblical text, and especially even to mimic that style by talking a good deal about one's own personal narrative.[14] (As if in public a person can be both perceptive and honest about one's own life story.) I question the value of such attempts to amplify and enliven the biblical text, at least as practiced by many preachers, whose detailed digressions waste time that might be spent in preaching the continual comfort and the contemporary challenges that are offered to believers by the presence of Christ in the community of faith.

Sometimes the intention of such preaching is to support the lean biblical account with extra-biblical historical details. Perhaps some preachers imagine each such historical detail as one of the flying buttresses shoring up the medieval cathedral of the faith. One recent published sermon for Easter day was crafted as if spoken by Magdalene, in which she explains why she refused to marry the man who had been chosen by her father.[15] Presumably this preacher uses the sermon in part to educate the assembly about first-century Palestine. Another recent study of Mary Magdalene states, "Luke does not indicate how old Mary was when she met Jesus, but she was most likely in her twenties, slightly older than he."[16] (Mary Magdalene's age? What is this?) With the evangelist writing in the late 80s for his Greco-Roman Christian community, we ought not expect to find in Luke's Gospel or the Acts of the Apostles much accurate biography about Jesus' inner circle half a century prior.

Perhaps such elaborations of the biblical narratives intend to enliven the proclamation of the Scriptures, a goal which might be achieved by more proficient lectoring. If the idea is to lighten the proclamation with humor, I question whether the assembly's laughter, trained by televised laugh tracks, is a trustworthy indicator of successful homiletical comedy. (With a world filled to overflowing with suffering, we attend worship to be entertained?) But critical biblical studies notwithstanding, popular fiction and film continue to depict Magdalene as a whore, and preachers must decide what to do with this popular misinterpretation. Do preachers ignore the tradition of Magdalene as an enticing sinner, or somehow salvage it for the twenty-first century?

I am glad to hear that a preaching style in which a narrative about Magdalene is received as especially appropriate for women seems to have abated. To make biblical characters into gender-specific models cuts in half their usefulness in reminding the entire baptized community of its failings and in forming us all as Christians. While I am grateful that the Revised Common Lectionary includes more stories about women—for example, replacing at the Easter Vigil Exodus 15:1 with 15:20-21, Moses's song replaced by Miriam's victory dance, and including during the weeks of Easter the stories in Acts about Dorcas, Lydia, and the fortune-teller—we ought not be naive about such narratives. Biblical accounts of women, whether inspiring or dreadful, were given their place in the communal record, usually by men, decades and even centuries after their historical setting. Welcome as they are, they cannot be taken as "women's stories," if this implies that they are historically accurate narratives of the experiences of women or were authored by women. A story about women is not necessarily a women's story.

Perhaps it was my initial academic training in literature that encourages me to appreciate preaching that, rather than elaborating on biblical characters, immerses the assembly in the biblical images. Not only boys benefit from the adventures of Huck Finn: the river journey invites all of Twain's readers to climb onto a raft. At the Vigil, we are all Moses, called to free those who are oppressed, and we all are Miriam, dancing on the safe side of the sea. The Bible was trans before we were. We are all Mary Magdalene, released from seven demons and traveling the road with Jesus, all standing at the foot of the cross and witnessing to Christ's resurrection.[17]

It is my formation as a Lutheran that makes me relatively fierce about the content of preaching. Martin Luther taught that Christ is truly present in the proclamation of the Word no less than in the bread and wine of the Eucharist, and thus I am resistant to proposals that construe the sermon as a time for comparative Gospels study, first-century historical research, imaginative storytelling, assembly entertainment, participatory conversation, or personal disclosure. I, however, trust that in many of the four thousand sermons I have heard, the Spirit of God was present and active, any appearances to the contrary notwithstanding. Some of you women and men enact this witness by preaching at the Sunday assembly. I do not, since I have not been ordained by my church body to do so. Rather, I rely on those who offer themselves up as voices of the Spirit of the risen Christ to fulfill this communal liturgical task.

By the way, in Year C of the three-year ecumenical lectionaries, the gospel on the Sunday between July 17 and 23, and thus the Sunday near to Mary Magdalene's Day on July 22, is Luke 10:38-42, the narrative of Mary of Bethany and her sister Martha serving a meal to Jesus. Mary of Magdalene, Mary of Bethany? I hear Pope Gregory laughing from the grave.

Let me conclude with one more quote from the twelfth-century *Life of Saint Mary Magdalene*: "Happy is the one who has heard all this concerning Mary Magdalene with pleasure."[18]

Chapter

Revering the Cross with Radegund

Radegund was a Thuringian princess, born in about 520, who at age twelve was kidnapped as war booty by an army of marauding Franks from the west. Although the family of her birth was pagan, she became a devout Christian over her teenage years. In 540 she was forced to become one of the six wives (plus one concubine) of King Clothair I of Merovingian Gaul—a monarch who was quite clearly not a fully formed Christian. After the king in 550 murdered Radegund's brother, who was her only living family member, she left the court and, urging the bishop, despite the objections of the king, to veil her, she became a nun. In 557 she founded the Abbey of the Holy Cross, a monastery at Poitiers in France that became a center for piety, charity, and refuge for women. She required all the nuns in her convent to become literate. Most significant for later centuries of Christians, she brought to her convent the famed Roman poet Venantius Fortunatus, who became her secretary, friend, and, fortunately for us, her hymnwriter-on-demand. She died on August 13, 587. She is buried in the crypt of the basilica in Poitiers, and when I visited that grand church, a woman was kneeling in prayer at her sarcophagus.

A recent persuasive biographical study describes Radegund's mastery of the art of wielding power.[1] Born to a royal family, married into a stronger royal court, a woman of considerable wealth and extraordinary learning, she could manage power to her own benefit, as exemplified in the establishment of her convent against the wishes of her husband, the king. Yet as a devout

Christian, she turned that power into the dictates of the gospel, becoming renowned for her sanctity, alms-giving, care for the sick and poor, peace-making diplomacy, and personal asceticism. She was honored for washing the feet of lepers, and stories of her miracles abound. So it was that she became an exemplar of the paradox of Christ: she renounced her crown in order to live with her sisters in suffering and servanthood—she did not serve as abbess—and thus she reigned as a truer queen than the secular court could ever cultivate.

The most impressive example of Radegund's exercise of power came in her eventually negotiating for her convent a fragment of the True Cross. This was a time of reverence for relics—when it was thought that the power of Christ or of the sainted dead could be transferred from its original place to distant churches and local shrines, or to a cabinet of a wealthy collector, thus spreading worldwide the blessed aura of the faith. By securing this icon of the crucifixion, Radegund linked her own Poitiers to the most prominent Christian centers of Jerusalem and Rome, and she appropriated for herself something of the status of that earlier Empress Helena, who in 324, according to legend, had on a religious archaeological expedition unearthed the True Cross at Golgotha. Disseminated around the Christian world, splinters of this wood—along with, undoubtedly, thousands of reasonable facsimiles—brought to the devout a proximity to holiness, as if each sliver was a matchstick that had been lighted by the resurrection. Although the image of the cross had served Emperor Constantine as a sign of military conquest, at Radegund's convent the fragment of the cross signified her rejection of worldly authority toward holiness and charity, from men on the battlefield to women in the convent library.

In celebration of the True Cross enshrined at Radegund's abbey, Fortunatus penned several of his masterpieces, *Pange lingua gloriosi* and *Vexilla regis prodeunt*, poems that are still sung by Christian assemblies as the hymns "Sing, My Tongue, the Glorious Battle"[2] and "The Royal Banners Forward Go."[3]

Although these hymns carry some imagery of military might, they are in the main praise of the cross as a beauteous and fruitful tree. The cross is revered, not as an instrument of torture—as if misery is what God intends for Jesus and for us all—but rather as the paradoxical sign of the mystery of divine transformation of death into life. These poems of Fortunatus now head a lengthy list of Christian hymns composed over the centuries that praise the cross as the archetypal tree of life. As the community of Stanbrook Abbey sings it,[4]

> O cross of Christ, immortal tree
> On which our Savior died,
> The world is sheltered by your arms
> That bore the crucified.

My favorite such hymn is "There in God's Garden," translated from the seventeenth-century Hungarian: "Tree of all knowledge, Tree of all compassion, Tree of all beauty . . . There on its branches see the scars of suffering. . . . Yet, look! It lives! Its grief has not destroyed it, nor fire consumed it."[5] In such song, Christians acclaim the mysteries of the death and resurrection of Christ to be the salvation of human life.

Hmm, how exactly does that work? What's the pathway from Calvary to every assembly of the baptized, to the heart of each believer?

There have been three dominant answers to this question, theories of atonement that propose a way to think about how it is that Christ's death brings us life.[6] According to Irenaeus in the second century, salvation is like a battlefield in which, although Satan had assumed victory at the crucifixion, the empty tomb at Easter proved that Christ had indeed conquered the devil. Given the combative nature of the decades of the Reformation, Martin Luther was drawn to this image. (See "the deeper magic from before the dawn of time" in C. S. Lewis's allegory *The Lion, the Witch, and the Wardrobe*.)[7] Centuries later, Anselm offered a quite different picture of salvation as a medieval law court: our sins had offended the honor of the Almighty; yet although guilty, we had been vindicated by God our Judge because Jesus had substituted for us, bearing our punishment. The Western focus on personal sin has ingrained this image too deep in us to extract. (Consider the treason of Edmund in, once again, *The Lion, the Witch, and the Wardrobe*.)[8] Then came Abelard, with a suggestion resonant with individual emotion: Christ serves as our loving example in living the resurrected life. As Mechthild of Magdeburg wrote in 1250, "I cannot dance, O Lord, unless you lead me. If you want me to leap with abandon, you must intone the song!"[9] In the nineteenth century, Friedrich Schleiermacher utilized this theory so as to encourage the moral life of the believer. Each of these theories has both attractive and disconcerting features, and thus none has become the church's sole explanation as to the means to our salvation.

However, since the second century, the church has witnessed also a fourth theory of atonement, displayed in the work of its artists, preached in its profound homilies, sung in the stanzas of its hymns: the cross of Christ is paradoxically the tree of life. I wonder whether Radegund knew of an anonymous third-century homily, of which this quote is a short excerpt:

> This cross is the tree of my eternal salvation nourishing and delighting me. I take root in its roots, I am extended in its branches. This is my nourishment when I am hungry, my fountain when I am thirsty, my covering when I am stripped, for my leaves are no longer fig leaves but the breath of life. This is my safeguard when I fear God, my support when I falter, my prize when I enter combat, and my trophy when I triumph. This is my narrow path, my steep way. This is the ladder of Jacob, the way of angels, at the summit of which the Lord is truly established. This is my tree, wide as the firmament, the pillar of the universe, the support of the whole world. Its top touches the highest heavens, its roots are planted in the earth. It is wholly in all things and in all places.[10]

This universe-tree, nearly ubiquitous in the symbol systems of human cultures and religions, is readily available to our imagination, and surprised by baptism, we see the cross transfigured into this very tree.

I have found this tree-cross throughout Christian practice.[11] On my wall is an El Salvadorian folk crucifix: superimposed on the cross is a tree, and on the tree is Christ, his arms becoming branches and his feet roots, with all the birds of the air nesting in the leaves. My favorite monumental image of the tree-cross is the thirteenth-century mosaic in the apse in San Clemente, Rome: from the crucifix flow the four rivers of Eden; the deer from Psalm 42 are lapping up the water; Mary and John flank Christ on the cross, and the birds of the air rest on the cross, the hand of God is above the cross, and in the fifty swirls that grow out from the tree-cross (the fifty days of Easter?) are tiny depictions of animals and saints—all of God's creation made new in the life of the cross. One fascinating proposal suggests that the medieval Christianization of the Nordic lands benefited by parallels made between the cross and Yggdrasil, with the vine designs transferred from the pagan tree to the cross, even the architecture of the stave churches inviting the new Christians to enter into the faith as into the mythical tree.[12]

And for children is the enchanting medieval legend of the tree that grew out from the grave of Adam, became a miraculous healing planting, and eventually served as the wood of the cross, in *The True Cross,* illustrated by Brian Wildsmith.[13]

To the characteristic images of Christ as a conquering warrior, the willing substitute for our punishment, or the loving leader of the faithful, we can say, try this: In the incarnation, God turns all human logic inside out. The divine becomes human, the monarch of the universe becomes a Jewish peasant, and in the paradox of mercy, what we thought was death has become life for all. By faith, strengthened by the spirit of the community of Christ, we see that the despicable torture stake of Roman execution is—to our amazement—a flowering tree in the Easter garden, its fruits ripening all year long, its leaves granting healing to the nations. Drops of blood glisten as valuable gems; a queen becomes a nun; a splinter of wood enlivens the faith of many. What our minds cannot fathom, our imaginations can suggest: the cross is the tree of life.

Perhaps our imagining the cross as the tree of life can bring some atonement to the human misuse of God's creation of which we are finally aware. It is only recently that the faithful have considered the cosmic damage that the church's standard reading of Genesis 1:26—"let them have dominion over the fish of the sea, . . . and over all the wild animals of the earth"— has occasioned. In our time, the True Cross might be not a sliver broken off from some dry branch, but rather the majestic living tree of the divine Spirit of continual creation that promises to restore healing to our earth. Such a cross can exemplify God's gift of life and beckon us to nurture all the trees we are given. You're a Christian? Plant a tree.

The three-year ecumenical lectionary brings us this tree-cross.[14] On the Baptism of our Lord, Year A, and on the second Sunday of Easter, Year C, the Acts readings refer to the cross as a tree. On the first Sunday of Advent in Year C, an ancient poem presents us with the Jesse tree, sprouting forth a righteous branch. Eden's tree of the knowledge of good and evil meets its match on the sixth Sunday of Easter in Year C, when at least in the Revised Common Lectionary, we are finally granted access to the tree of life in the city of God. And during June in Year B, when the Gospel is the illogical parable in which the scrubby annual mustard bush gets likened to the archetypal tree of life, the first reading is an oracle from Ezekiel, in which God promises to "bring low the high tree and make high the low tree"; "in the shade of its branches will nest winged creatures of every kind." Several times through the year we join together in Psalm 1, and for Christians, the tree planted by the river is the cross marking our baptism. And, of course, in midsummer in Year C we are shown the "fruit of the Spirit," love, joy, peace, patience, kindness, generosity, faithfulness, gentleness, self-control. In the nineteenth century, prints of this Tree of Life, its fruits labeled according to this passage in Galatians, were popular among American Protestants. I like especially the one by E. B. and E. C. Kellogg: in the urban scene depicted in the foreground, people are engaging in rather disreputable behavior, despite the efforts of several Methodist preachers who are summoning the sinners to salvation, while in the background Christ hangs on the fruited tree in walled city of God.

What of the cross in your sanctuary? Would its depiction elicit reverence? Some churches display a classic crucifix that is so stereotypical as to be little more than wallpaper; other churches post only a totally plain "Easter" cross. Some worship spaces are loaded with cheesy crosses, embroidered onto paraments or glued onto felt banners. Perhaps when next your congregation mourns the death of one of your little old ladies, you can memorialize her by commissioning a processional cross that is also tree of life, and as that cross leads us into worship and out again to the streets, we all turn to honor this vivifying sign of salvation.

There is no extant quote from Radegund with which to conclude this essay, but we do have the tree-of-life stanza by her companion Fortunatus resounding in our worship spaces.

> Bend your boughs, O tree of glory,
> your relaxing sinews bend . . .
> and the Lord of heav'nly beauty
> gently on your arms extend.

> Faithful cross, true sign of triumph,
> be for all the noblest tree;
> none in foliage, none in blossom,
> none in fruit your equal be;
> symbol of the world's redemption,
> for your burden makes us free.[15]

Please join me and Radegund in revering this tree, the cross that offers life to the world.

Chapter 14

Singing Hymns with Philipp Nicolai

P hilipp Nicolai, a late sixteenth-century German Lutheran pastor, was both castigated and beloved for his extraordinary ability with words. He was highly educated, with a doctorate in theology from the University of Wittenberg. He became infamous for his role in the polemical battles that raged between Lutherans and Roman Catholics and between Lutherans and the Reformed, and several of his transfers from one clerical position to another resulted from the unwonted vehemence of his rhetoric and his excessive belligerence in doctrinal controversies. Here is the title of one of his anti-Reformed essays: "The Driving Away of the Indefensible, Vain, and Dung-Putrid Deliverance Which the Calvinists of Unna Have Allowed to Go Forth Against the Hammer-blow of the Divine Word in the Controverted Article of the Ubiquity."[1] (Note: polite speech is not a bad thing.)

However, when he was a pastor in several congregations and for a time a court preacher in Altwildungen, Nicolai's preaching was so eloquent that he was called a second Chrysostom. While ministering in a congregation in Unna during the 1597 outbreak of the plague, where 1300 people died over a six-month period, he conducted as many as thirty funerals a day, and he was revered for how he spoke comfort to those who suffered. As he himself wrote, "During the entire time of the plague I put all disputes in the back of my mind with prayer and with the praiseworthy reflection upon eternal life."[2] He died, only fifty-two years old, on October 26, 1608.

So why might we think of this man—both vituperative and compassionate—on a Sunday? Among his voluminous publications were two hymns for which he wrote the text and composed the tune. Both of these hymns are so superlative that they have been honored by subsequent centuries as the Queen and the King of Chorales. The enduring vitality of hymn texts and tunes as profound as his deserve our continuing esteem and, at least once a year, the full voices of our assemblies.

The honorific Queen of Chorales has been granted to his *Wie schön leuchtet*, translated variously into English as "O Morning Star, How Fair and Bright," "How Brightly Shines the Morning Star," or "How Lovely Shines the Morning Star." The Morning Star is, of course, Christ, from Revelation 22:16. (Would the assembly know this?) Nicolai prefaced his text with this comment, "A spiritual bride-song of the believing soul of Jesus Christ, her heavenly bridegroom."[3] The text presents itself as the worshipers' love song to Christ, who is our bridegroom, *mein Schatz* (my treasure, sweetheart), the *schöne Freudenkrone* (the beautiful crown of joy). The text is a riff on the parable in Matthew 25:1-13 of the wise and foolish bridesmaids, with whom we wait to greet the coming Christ.

Nicolai's seven stanzas present a scrapbook of biblical references that describe and laud the presence of Christ in the believer's heart, in word and sacrament, in the community of the faithful, throughout life, and in and after death. A dominant image throughout the stanzas is the light of the divine, a flame that ignites the believers' hearts into gratitude, despite the misery around them and the suffering they experience. The imagery of light has tied this hymn in Lutheran practice not only to the Sunday of the parable of the bridesmaids, but also to the festival of the Epiphany. Also, the hymn's evocation of divine love led in the past to its popularity as the primary hymn at Lutheran weddings.

Nicolai's text exemplifies how Protestants utilized the marriage imagery found in the Scriptures. Through the twelfth to fifteenth centuries, during which time the Western tradition

lauded celibacy as the preferred life choice, the biblical bride
came more and more to be interpreted as the individual soul
united in love with Christ.[4] But Protestants revived the earlier
Christian pattern of interpreting the bride as the whole church,
and in sermon and song they borrowed language from Psalm
45, the Song of Songs, the parables of the wedding feast, Ephesians 5, and Revelation 21–22 to describe the mystical union
between Christ and the gathered church that is effected through
the Word and nurtured through the Eucharist. Reformation
theologians stressed that the believer's access to the divine
came about solely through the gift of the Savior. Since, at least
until recent times, a cultural stereotype described marriage as
the bond between a passive subservient woman and her active
lord and master, Protestant emphasis on "grace alone" could
make good use of the scriptural language about the bond of
marriage between the lowly female and the dominant male. In
our time, this marriage imagery is justifiably problematic. As
a wife, I am not a hopeless and helpless underling of my husband, and I can appreciate that some women—and indeed some
men—could choose to take a pass while this hymn is being
sung. (During which hymns do you take a pass?)

But this is only one example of the perennial difficulty with
biblical metaphors: which images absolutely frost you? (You
exit the room, freezing.) I suggest that our use of the biblical
image of Christ as bridegroom be celebrated, oh, perhaps twice
a year, and that on those Sundays other metaphors offer a welcome balance. Christ as bridegroom, Christ as river; Christ as
king, Christ as servant. It is paramount that metaphors retain
their "no." Christ is not a bridegroom; God is not a father. In
religion, a literalized metaphor becomes what the Bible calls an
idol. The struggle in the church is whether to agree about when
the imagery itself is being worshiped, rather than the mysterious
merciful Trinity who is hidden behind the metaphor.

A key to what seems to have been the genuine affections of
the author-composer Nicolai is hidden in an acrostic in the
German text. Nicolai served for several years as tutor to

Wilhelm Ernst, Count and Lord of Waldeck, the first letters of whose name and title in German were W, E, G, V, H, Z, and W. In Nicolai's text, the opening words of the seven stanzas are the following: *Wie, Ei, Geuss, Von, Herr, Zwingt*, and *Wie*. His student Wilhelm died of plague in 1597, and Nicolai first published this text in 1599, hiding in his magisterial composition his memorial to his dear student.

Hidden away in Nicolai's fourth stanza is another brilliance that cannot be replicated in an English translation. Between the stanza's first twenty-one words and its final twenty-one words is the central line of this central stanza. "Dein Wort, dein Geist, dein Leib und Blut," literally translated "your word, your Spirit, your body and blood," is the pivot of the entire hymn text,[5] as it was the crux of Nicolai's spirituality—that through the Spirit in Scripture and Eucharist is the union of Christ with the church.

And if you want another indication of what makes this hymn a masterpiece, here is how the text appears when printed as the poem it is:[6]

> O Morning Star, how fair and bright!
> You shine with God's own truth and light,
> aglow with grace and mercy!
> Of Jacob's line, King David's son,
> our Lord and Savior, you have won
> our hearts to serve you only!
> Lowly,
> holy!
> Great and glorious,
> all victorious,
> rich in blessing!
> Rule and might o'er all possessing!

The stanza takes the form of a chalice—like the one from which all Lutheran worshipers would have drunk at Communion.

Now to the King of Chorales, *Wachet auf*, in English variously "Wake, Awake," "Wake, O Wake," or "Sleepers, Wake!"

This hymn is also an appropriation of the parable of the wise and foolish bridesmaids, but the emphasis has moved from the love song of the beloved to the procession of all the guests into the marriage feast, although much of this marriage imagery has been lost in current English translations. The stanzas superimpose the wedding celebration of Matthew 25 on the prophet's cry in Isaiah 51, 52, and 62: together we watch for the Messiah and laud the arrival of the Blessed One. The banquet hall has become the entire walled city of Jerusalem. The third stanza moves us into yet greater dimensions: assisted by the imagery of Revelation 19-22, we all together enter the presence of God at the end of time and sing with angels around the throne. The imagery of one loving couple has expanded to embrace the whole company of heaven.

And once more, Count Wilhelm is present. The opening words of the chorale's three stanzas are *Wachet*, *Zion*, and *Gloria*, which is Nicolai's student's title "Graf zu Waldeck" hiding in reverse order. In several recent translations of this hymn, this tribute to the heart of Nicolai remains: the words Wake, Zion, and Gloria/Glory begin the stanzas.[7]

The tune of this King of Chorales captures the majesty of a stately coronation march. Do, mi, so—so so so la so: here's the simplicity of excellence. Scientific studies have determined that group singing, which sadly our culture seldom engages in, causes the release of endorphins, which bring about the sensation of pleasure, and of oxytocin, which alleviates anxiety and stress. Even those persons who can't carry the tune are found to benefit psychologically when participating in communal song.[8] And in many churches, everyone stands to sing, honoring the wisdom of John Wesley, whose delightful "Directions for Singing" urged his congregations, "Beware of singing as if you were half dead, or half asleep. . . . Be no more afraid of your voice now, nor more ashamed of its being heard, than when you sung the songs of Satan."[9] In some matters it is advisable for the churches to join with cultural practices, but in other matters the church is urged to resist contemporary trends: so although Americans seldom sing together, even burdened with an unsingable national anthem, Christians do.

Christian tradition gives us varying genres for assembly song, from medieval chant to strophic hymns to calls-and-responses to revival sing-alongs. Philipp Nicolai is an honored representative of the chorale tradition, in which the texts are complex poems, sustained over a number of stanzas, that develop biblical metaphors toward individual meditation and communal unity. Fortunatus's hymns on the cross, "Sing, My Tongue, the Glorious Battle" and "The Royal Banners Forward Go," Kiraly Imre's "There in God's Garden," Martin Luther's Christmas ballad "From Heaven Above to Earth I Come"[10]— these, too, are hymns into which we enter for five to ten minutes; the hymn contains us; you can't skip a stanza or two; you have to go the whole way. These hymns are not superficial ditties: they are adventures in spirituality. If service planners are watching the clock, these hymns may end up shelved in ecclesiastical museums, next to the dove-shaped ciboria. But if the service planners hope that at least one hymn each Sunday is chosen for the lifelong worshipers—those faithful believers who know their Bible, those readers who enjoy elevated prose— then texts such as these by Nicolai come to our rescue. To make hymn-singing better, sing better hymns.

Let us look to November in Year A when the gospel is Matthew 25:1-13, the parable of the wise and foolish bridesmaids. Which hymns might we appoint, songs through which we celebrate that we have been joined to God as at a marriage? (Remember the Exultet of the Easter Vigil: "This is the night in which heaven and earth are joined, things human and things divine.")[11] For we are the wise and the foolish bridesmaids, the prophet Isaiah, and the multitude around the throne. For the throne of God is here, in the bread and wine on the altar, in our hands and in our mouths. I hope that your assembly will choose several of the following for the songs on that Sunday:[12] the African American spiritual "Soon and Very Soon"; Paul Gerhardt's "Soul, Adorn Yourself with Gladness"; the eighteenth-century hymn "Rejoice, Rejoice, Believers"; Isaac Watts's "Come, We That Love the Lord"; Fanny Crosby's gospel song "Blessed Assurance"; the South African cry "Freedom Is Coming"; the Taizé chant "Wait for the Lord"; John Bell's "Send Out Your Light," sounding our way from the Iona community. But I urge—how many of my readers agree with me?—that at least one of the hymns on that Sunday be the German chorale *Wachet Auf*, and that at least some of your assembly will read in the worship folder about the author-composer, his thirty funerals a day, the memorial to his beloved student, and the many biblical references that turned Nicolai's nasty tongue into praise. As some of us sing our hearts out, those worshipers who are not yet converts to such assembly song can spend those minutes, watching those of us for whom such song is a valued ritual formative of our faith.

Join with me in Nicolai's original final lines of *Wachet Auf*,[13] a conclusion that generations of translators have found no way to render. (Did they perhaps judge it too delightful for church on Sunday?) This hymn was composed for use during November, when the congregation was looking forward to singing Christmas carols. Nicolai knew that no single language can say all our praise, no Sunday of the liturgical year is untouched by the remainder of the year. So he crafted a couplet in which the vernacular German first resorted to babble and then relied on ancient Latin:

> *Das sind wir froh, i-o, i-o,*
> *Ewig in dulci jubilo.*

Can we sing like this with Philipp Nicolai?

Chapter *15*

Honoring Images with John of Damascus

J ohn of Damascus, about whose biography little is known,
lived during one of the church's episodes of iconoclasm.
The historical record has not established precisely why,
from 726 to 843, several Byzantine emperors sought to eliminate religious images from Orthodox churches and throughout
Eastern devotional life. The influence of neighboring aniconic
Islam was perhaps in part responsible, although a horrendous
volcanic explosion may have suggested to some authorities
that God was angry with local worship practices. Enter John
of Damascus. It seems that the highly educated John had followed his father and his grandfather in a career in the fiscal
administration of the Islamic caliphate in Damascus, but in
about 706, John entered a monastery near Jerusalem, becoming
ordained in perhaps 735. He is honored as one of the fathers
of the Eastern church, and in the West the Golden Canon that
he composed for use on Easter Day and on the Sunday following is still sung as the hymns "The Day of Resurrection" and
"Come, You Faithful, Raise the Strain."[1] John is most revered
for his defense of the presence and veneration of images,
whether on what are now called "icons" or on vessels, fabrics,
mosaics, manuscript illuminations, even statues.[2] Most important are his three treatises "On the Divine Images," each of
which concludes with supporting citations from earlier Christian authorities upon which he comments.[3] He died in 749 on
December 4, and the commemoration of his life is kept by some
churches on that date.

John of Damascus opened his defense by distinguishing the veneration of worship that is granted only to God (*latria*) from the veneration of honor that is due to created matter (*dulia*). Honoring matter is an appropriate Christian activity, since through the incarnation God entered matter, within which God's being can be revered. Humans "see images in created things intimating to us dimly reflections of the divine," and John theorized that "through the senses a certain imaginative image is constituted in the front part of the brain and thus conveyed to the faculty of discernment and stored in the memory."[4] Just as God had commanded the Israelites to construct images of the cherubim, so for Christians the divine is glimpsed through both images from Scripture and depictions of the saints, whose lives show forth God. John asks, "What is the purpose of the image? . . . The image was devised to guide us to knowledge and to make manifest and open what is hidden, certainly for our profit and well-doing and salvation, so that, as we learn what is hidden from things recorded and noised abroad, we are filled with desire and zeal for what is good, and avoid and hate the opposite, that is, what is evil."[5] As Christ is the icon of God, so the material world can serve as an icon of the divine. To venerate the icon is to honor Christ is to worship God.[6]

John of Damascus wrote that the church ought never attempt to depict the incorporeal God. And I agree with him: the wall painting covering the chancel and the front of the nave in the Lutheran church of my childhood that depicted not only archangels, angels, and recognizable deceased congregation members, but also each of the three persons of the Trinity, was not a good idea. (Don't get me started.) And although I know of one eminent feminist theologian who admired the Throne of Grace image, in which God is depicted as an old man on a throne, the crucified Christ on God's lap, and a dove hovering above, such a depiction of the incorporeal God worries me as being dangerously close to making for ourselves an idol.

However, John did advocate depicting biblical metaphors and the church's saints to assist us in imagining the divine. We need "familiar and natural points of reference,"[7] for example by depicting the sun, or a fountain, or a rose. John wrote that in Exodus 3 that the burning bush is an image of Mary.[8] So it is that in the breathtaking Orthodox church of St. Herman of Alaska in Tapiola, Finland, completed in 2008 with icons entirely covering its walls and ceiling, the iconographer Alexander Wikström depicted the burning bush, within which is Mary and the child Jesus, who is holding the scroll of the Word.[9] In that church, the saints, through whom we see something of heaven, flank the nave, women on one side, men on the other. Its icon depicting Andrei Rublev shows the iconographer holding his icon of the Trinity. John wrote that churches should include also "images of the future,"[10] and in the Anastasis at St. Herman, similar to the renowned wall painting in the Chora Orthodox church outside of Istanbul, Turkey, Christ tramples down the doors of Hades and looks straight out to us as, with one arm extended to each, he pulls up both Eve and Adam out of death, thus anticipating our own equal opportunity resurrection.

John also wrote that churches should include "images of what is past . . . for the benefit of those who behold them later."[11] Listen to Martin Luther preaching on Easter Day and praising the sanctuary's image of Christ conquering hell: "Since we cannot think of anything or understand it without pictures, it is fine and proper that people look at it in accord with the Word."[12] Following Martin Luther's practice, most traditional Lutherans, as distinct from Calvinists, did not reject imagery in their churches.[13] Nor after the Reformation did they whitewash their medieval buildings. If you travel northwest up from Uppsala, Sweden, you can wonder at the fifteenth-century churches, still used each Sunday, which were entirely painted with biblical narratives of the life of Christ flanked by parallel stories from the Old Testament and signed by an "Albertus Pictor."[14]

In one of my favorite churches in all the world, Lutherans in Lohja, Finland, worship in the late medieval sanctuary in which, entering under the image of the Jesse tree, we see, encircling us around the nave, depictions of the creation of the world, the fall, the annunciation, the entire story of the life of Christ, the resurrection, and the Last Judgment. On the ceiling are the Old Testament stories that parallel the narratives of the New; and on the four sides of the pillars are the saints; and throughout the room, branches of the Jesse tree, inserting us into the past, benefiting us now.[15] Over the altar we see the Israelites receiving the manna. What's not to admire in a tour de force such as this? When one hears that the church building is the house not of God but of God's people, I say, yes: God's people now, joined with God's people then.

I cheer at John's comment about formation of the young Christian: "How therefore shall we not depict in images what Christ our God endured for our salvation and his miracles, so that, when my son asks me, what is this? I shall say that God the Word became human and through him not only did Israel cross over the Jordan, but our whole nature was restored to ancient blessedness."[16] When I brought my preschool daughters to visit St. Patrick's Cathedral in New York City, they traced with their fingers the image of Elizabeth Seton on its bronze doors, which prompted me to tell them about her. By the way, in the eighth century, some men claimed that it was only "simpleminded" women who needed images, since they hadn't the brains to grasp theology. It was in fact the eighth-century Empress Irene and the ninth-century Empress Theodora whose efforts through and around their emperor husbands and sons successfully thwarted the iconoclasts; and in between was Empress Euphrosyne, from whom we learn never to underestimate the power of grandmothers to instill a spirituality into their dear little ones.[17] None of us now accuses women of being dim-witted, and I have never been a gender essentialist; however, I am not surprised that whoever attends children at worship and teaches them the faith at home advocates for imagery in the churches.

I am here not considering the interiors of monastic churches, since I, not being a nun, cannot judge what is best for them.[18]

Nor am I considering interfaith sacred spaces, the Rothko Chapels of the world, that mean to encourage a "journey into the unknown."[19] I am here not concerned with spaces that are shaped primarily to accommodate the contemporary search for the personally spiritual.[20] Rather, I am considering the room in which the Sunday assembly meets for word and sacrament, and that baptized assembly includes toddlers with their soft toys, recalcitrant teens, the aged with early dementia, those whose last catechesis was thirty years prior, as well as those who serve on the liturgy committee, those up-to-date on their theological reading, those recently returned from a spiritual retreat. What would John of Damascus say to us about the interior of such spaces?

It came to be that the second half of the twentieth century witnessed another of the church's episodes of iconoclasm. Admittedly, many church buildings, littered with junk, sorely needed a house-cleaning. Some sanctuaries were also filled with shrines intended for private devotion, as if the communal liturgy was only a distraction, and the primary intention of entering the building was homage to one's preferred saints. But perhaps in reaction to such religious clutter, and far indeed from the error of the adoration of images, many modern churches don't have any images at all. A significant influence toward contemporary aniconic worship spaces was the Bauhaus school of design, which taught that form follows function and that only what directly serves function is admissible to the form.[21] (So what is the function of a church building?) By questioning the sleek Bauhaus ideal, I do not mean to suggest that in our century we revert to neo-Gothic spaces. Rather, I ask: in our buildings, stunning in their contemporary design, what visuals would complement liturgical action and enhance baptismal identity? Even motels mimic family homes by placing images on the walls. How do we make our spaces into storytellers of the faith, "an opportunity for catechesis and spiritual renewal of the entire community"?[22] A second influence toward aniconic spaces was the twentieth-century aesthetic mandating that less is more. The photographs in recent publications praising modern church design show nothing on the walls, empty expanses up to high ceilings, one Quaker space after another, despite the use of these structures by sacramental churches.[23] Sheer white does not majesty make.

Nor can I concur that during a time when art is increasingly individualistic, abstract art solves our liturgical dilemma.[24] In one account of the fracas experienced in 1985 when the New York City Lutheran congregation Saint Peter's considered displaying an abstract expressionist triptych by Willem de Kooning behind the free-standing altar (thus transforming a contemporary flexible worship space into a medieval cathedral?), the commentator suggested that in our time churches do well to choose "the radically private world of a single artist . . . a highly abstract language."[25] However, I answer that not even a single Sunday's sermon ought to express the "radically private world" of the preacher. Nobody who visit galleries of contemporary art as regularly as I do is dismissive of abstract art. But in our eucharistic meeting halls, our Sunday homesteads, are de Kooning's swirls of color the best we can do? While a professor of religion at a Roman Catholic university, I would tour the university chapel with my classes. Its Stations of the Cross were abstract designs. My students, most of whom had attended eight to twelve years of Catholic schools, got zero out of these images. Once a student pointed to something that might be Veronica—hardly a comfort to a Bible reader like me. Simply said, the non-figurative abstractions of the passion could contribute nothing to the formation of my students as Christians.[26]

Few parishes are able, like St. Gregory of Nyssa in San Francisco, to commission a Mark Dukes to paint walls covered with dancing saints. But some have adequate resources for such a Christianizing of their worship space. In the 1940s, the artist Hugo Lous Mohr painted a full ceiling mural in the Lutheran cathedral of Oslo. The painting depicts the three articles of the Christian creed—Christ creating, Christ victorious, and Christ baptized in the Spirit—each image incorporating the tree of life, and this accomplished during the Nazi occupation of Norway.[27] I particularly like the stained-glass windows in the Lutheran cathedral in Visby, Sweden, completed in 1985: in the resurrection window, we see Mary who can only glimpse Christ, who is hidden by the leaves of an immense tree. From 1987, in the large chapel of a Presbyterian church in Grand Rapids, Michigan, is a twelve-foot-long stained-glass window designed by the Japanese artist Sadao Watanabe that depicts twelve biblical narratives of God's covenant: take that, Calvin.[28] The frown on Isaac's face as Abraham prepares the sacrifice is irresistible. Closer to the folk art of the fifteenth-century Nordic churches is St. Mark's Episcopal parish in Beaver Creek, North Carolina, where on the chancel wall is a fresco of the Last Supper painted during the 1970s in such a way that, given the empty space near to Christ at the table, we can insert ourselves into Maundy Thursday.

But there are ways smaller than these to fill our eyes and hearts with Christian visuals that are derived from Scriptures, infused with sacramental reference, and hallowed by the saints. "One selects and develops a repertoire of images, chosen both because they attract and because from them one receives visual messages that help one to visualize—to envision—personal and social transformation and thus to focus the energy of attention and affection with more clarity."[29] During Lent, the front and back of the worship folders of one assembly were plain solid purple. (Get it?) Banners can be designed as other than signposts. In one congregation, the Sunday school children drew pictures of the six days of creation and held them up during the first reading of the Easter Vigil, and for the seventh day, they all joined God in lying down for a rest. On the fourth Sunday of Lent, Year C, the Jesuit community of Caravita in Rome displayed a reproduction of Rembrandt's Prodigal Son in the worship space: I wonder how many assemblies are benefiting from the several online listings of images that correspond in some way to the lectionary selections.[30] Displaying such images is a worthy use of all those white walls.

One last story about my formation. In 1963, I attended a high school physics conference (physics? me?) at Yale University. I have two memories: in the university library was a sign banning all females from entering the posh reading room. (Can you believe that?) But in the museum was exhibited the baptistery of the Dura Europos house church, set up in three dimensions, with a tub-sized font and the famous wall art, searing into my consciousness the baptismal woman at the well.[31] In later years the exhibit was dismantled for restoration. Now, the wall art has been returned to the museum's walls, without the baptistery itself being replicated. Thus, the liturgical context is no longer evident. What in our post-Christian culture has been given floor space in Yale's museum is a reproduction of Dura's Mithraeum. (But the baptismal wall paintings are still worth seeing: bring your imagination with you.)

One more quote from John of Damascus: "I therefore reverence matter and I hold in respect and venerate that through which my salvation has come about. I reverence it not as God, but as filled with divine energy and grace."[32] Please join me in searching for and sharing with the Sunday assembly such images of divine energy and grace.

Reciting the Creed with Johannes Kepler

Johannes Kepler was born in 1571 in the German city of Weil der Stadt in the Holy Roman Empire into a noble family much reduced by financial difficulties. As a youth, Kepler wanted to enter the Lutheran ministry and at one point studied theology with a student of Luther's colleague Philipp Melanchthon. However, given that he was an extraordinary mathematical genius, he became instead the founder of modern astronomy. His prominence in the field of science rests primarily upon his discovery of the laws of planetary motion, the most important of which proved the elliptical, as opposed to a spherical, orbit of the planets around the sun. His proposal and its voluminous supporting data confirmed a heliocentric planetary system and solved some of the problems inherent in the theory of Copernicus.

Before the scientific revolution of the seventeenth century, study of the stars went hand in hand with astrology, and repeatedly over his career, Kepler had to rely on casting horoscopes to support his family, which came to include eleven children, five of whom survived childhood. He eventually rose to become imperial mathematician in the court of Emperor Rudolf II and his royal successors. Kepler applied his mind to a surprising array of issues: the specific musical tones generated by the planetary orbits (remember Plato's "music of the spheres"?); the hexagonal design of snowflakes; the volume of wine barrels; the function of the lens in the human eye; a perfected refracting telescope; a cosmically accurate calendar—

as well as the defense of his mother, a herbalist accused of witchcraft. He died in Regensburg, Bavaria, on November 15, 1630, during the height of the Thirty Years' War.

Kepler was a Lutheran who took his religion seriously. Due to the political compromise attempted in Europe as an amelioration of the religious controversies of the sixteenth century— "as the prince, so the people"—Kepler was legally forced to reside, and thus to secure employment, in an area with a religiously amenable head of state. He refused to become a Roman Catholic, which would have mitigated his professional—and thus financial—difficulties, instead moving from one employment to another to satisfy territorial religious requirements. Because he could not intellectually accept the precise language that delineated the doctrine of the real presence of Christ in Holy Communion as was articulated by orthodox Lutherans at his time, he was accused of being a Calvinist, and so was both denied participation in the Eucharist in his Lutheran church and refused an academic position at the Lutheran University of Tübingen, although he fiercely denied the Reformed teaching about predestination. (Is that more than you wanted to know about denominational branding?)

In his writings, Kepler repeatedly expressed his devout conviction that the triune God, who is rational and active, the source of light and life, had created an intelligible universe, the beauty and order of which were available to humankind for studied investigation. He saw his own work as probing the harmonious precision that he believed God had implanted in all things. To Kepler, contemplating the creation was one way that believers came to revere God, and he considered such attention to God's creation to be a Christian duty. He proposed a unique trinitarian depiction of the cosmos, in which the universe itself was created in the image of God. God the Father was likened to the central sun, God the Son was symbolized by the surfaces of the created spheres, and God the Spirit was exhibited in the force of the spaces between.[1] Thus for Kepler, even the structure of the solar system was Christian. Although some of his scientific treatises included extensive theological discussions, his publishers tended to delete such material from his work, as the modern scholarly world was bringing to a virtual halt the centuries of religious scholars—monks, priests—who had pioneered the field of Western science.

When faced with the many biblical passages that described a geocentric universe, Kepler argued that the Bible was a spiritual, but not a scientific, guide and was replete with metaphoric language: "Who is unaware that the allusion in Psalm 19 is poetical?"[2] He suggested that biblical speech represented the world as seen by the eye. He explained why in Genesis 1 the universe is described as "the heavens and the earth": "it is these two parts that chiefly present themselves to the sense of sight."[3] Of similar descriptions of the earth found in the psalms, Kepler wrote that the author "should not be judged to have spoken falsely, for the perception of the eyes also has its truth, well suited to the psalmodist's more hidden aim, the adumbration of the Gospel and also of the Son of God."[4] Throughout the Christian tradition, believers had described what they saw of God's creation with their own eyes, rather than what was being discovered scientifically with laboratory instruments, and this allowed the scientist Kepler to continue to honor Scripture and to pray the psalms. In the Lutheran church orders of his time, Luther's creedal hymn *Wir glauben all'* would have been sung by the assembly or the Nicene Creed chanted by the presider or the choir.[5] In either case, the creed invited Kepler's assent to ancient descriptions of the world as it had been viewed by earlier believers. Kepler's integrity concerning participation at worship suggests to us that he gave to the creed his assent.

Kepler on Sunday: let us face the question of creeds.

At Sunday liturgies in the twenty-first century, there is a diversity of practice concerning the use of creeds. We might categorize a wide range of texts as creeds: statements of faith that function in the liturgy, at baptisms, for controversy, for irenic purpose, for reforming purpose, as apologetics, as

church-founding, or as church-uniting.[6] However, the noun
"creed" usually designates not any statement of faith, most
certainly not a text made up last week by the current pastoral
staff (worshipers are supposed to affirm a creed that they have
never before seen?), but rather one of several fixed, approved,
and historic statements of doctrine that speak authoritatively
from the past. Because of considerable discussion about whether
such texts continue to proclaim Christian belief in our time in
any meaningful way, it is often the case that creeds are omitted
from the assembly's worship, even in those denominations that
previously advocated their use. For although the assembly's
recitation of a formal statement of doctrine is a most appropriate response to the proclamation of the Word, it can be argued
that interceding for the world, sharing the peace of Christ, offering gifts for the needy, and participating in the Eucharist are
more profound ways than a creed for the assembly to say its
Yes to the gospel, without recourse to the arcane terminology
of previous centuries.

Liturgical theologians have demonstrated that the creed is
a late addition to Sunday worship. Yet for me, the past
informs—but does not dictate—the present and the future. I
wish to encourage a continuing use of the classic ecumenical
creeds as feasible curbs to demarcate the Christian roadway,
especially in a culture where it is deemed acceptable to believe
any old thing you want to believe today and to change your
mind tomorrow—since what you believe actually doesn't
much matter. Indeed, even if absent on Sunday, the language
of the creed will likely be part of the sacrament of baptism,
hidden in hymn stanzas, sung in the *Gloria in Excelsis*, cited in
historic prayers, studied in confirmation class, or featured in
interdenominational dialogue. In one way or another, at least
the Apostles' Creed, begun in the second century, and the
Niceno-Constantinopolitan Creed from the fourth century
continue to echo among the baptized. Here we can wave fare-
well to the sixth-century ecumenical creed, called the Athanasian, which the churches of my childhood read aloud each

Trinity Sunday.[7] It is perhaps not its lengthy repetition of trinitarian characteristics—"the Father incomprehensible, the Son incomprehensible, and the Holy Ghost incomprehensible, and yet they are not three Incomprehensibles, but one Incomprehensible" (what's not to enjoy, slogging through this!)—but the harshness of its final dictum, "which except a man believe faithfully and firmly, he cannot be saved," that has brought about its justifiable retirement from Sunday worship.

What are, however, some problematic phrases in those creeds that might still be part of your liturgical practice? In both the Apostles' and the Nicene Creeds, Christians affirm that Christ "is seated at the right hand of the Father." The earliest Christian use of this phrase to describe the risen Christ is found in Romans 8:34 and is repeated in Matthew, Mark, Luke, Acts, Ephesians, Colossians, and Hebrews—although, interestingly, not in any Johannine writings, despite their preference for symbolic speech. The phrase relies on an ancient picture of the universe: that the world has three layers; that God dwells in its top layer, "the heavens"; that God as sovereign of all things is the primordial father; that God sits upon a throne; that the risen Christ is as it were God's prime minister, or heir apparent, sitting to the right of God in the throne room, since in human speech for millennia "the right" is the preferred side of power. Two hundred years before Kepler, Julian of Norwich struggled to make sense of this phrase: "But it is not ment that the sonne sitteth on the right hand beside as one man sitteth by another in this life—for ther is no such sitting, as to my sight, in the trinity. But he sitteth on his faders right honde: that is to sey, right in the hyest nobilite of the faders joy."[8] Of this "right hand of the Father," as a Lutheran I can offer at least this: that thanks to Luther's cosmologically brilliant teaching about christological ubiquity, I recognize that "the right hand of God" is everywhere.

There is also the creedal imagery of the royal throne room. Kepler was spared the leap of language back into the time of kings: indeed, he was employed by the emperor. In our time, some Christians reciting the creeds are living under powerful monarchs, whether benign or horrendous; some Christians reside down the block from their figurehead royals; some claim the populace itself to be the nation's sovereign power. Yet recent political campaigns demonstrate that even citizens of democracies maintain, perhaps unconsciously, the myth of the crown,[9] imagining a president to have the power of a monarch and assuming that this authority will somehow improve their lives—which only shows that the legends about King Arthur trump historical knowledge as to how actual monarchs functioned with minimal regard for the welfare of their underlings. I say that an unexamined myth is not worth honoring: we should scrutinize the myths, searching out their truths and their lies. But perhaps most people are untroubled by a king reigning in their fantasy, concurring that the storybook figure and his beautiful consort can be borrowed on Sunday morning. By the way, this divine metaphor got overused in English-language hymns because "king" rhymes with "sing," as in, for example, Francis's Canticle of Brother Sun, sometimes rendered "All Creatures of our God and King," despite the fact that the original did not refer to God as a king.[10]

Can we be helped by Kepler's proposal that much historic spirituality is worded according to how we see, at least in our mind's eye? The creeds rely on sight lines: that God created "heaven and earth"; that the relationship between God and Jesus is like that between a father and a son; that on the third day Christ "rose again"; that we look for "the resurrection" at the end of time—resurrection being quite other than the immortality of the soul, which is a far more believable and intellectually respectable proposal to entertain. Outside worship, our speech is characterized by sight lines, as we look "up" to the "sky" after "the sun goes down"; even astronomers speak as they see. But I cannot rest peacefully with such creedal archaisms, unless our parish catechesis teaches, not once, but repeatedly—perhaps in adult classes on Bible and doctrine, or in explanations printed in the service folder, perhaps graciously illumined during preaching, or apparent in newly composed hymn texts—that Christian language is imagery that is doing the best that it can to speak of what is beyond words.

Yet it remains difficult for me to rest peacefully, for I know persons who have exited the church because of the aura of facticity that is painted over such phrases. To these persons, such speech is babble, senseless hocus-pocus, the memory of magical intent with no transformational wonder-working genuinely available for their lives. Responding to such people, I have come to advocate that we lay aside the more philosophically abstruse Nicene Creed for use at only the rarest occasions, while we continue to recite the baptismal Apostles' Creed, appointed with wisdom, taught with care, recited with respect. I like to think of being bonded with Kepler, as he plotted the orbit of Mars, assenting to that same creed, committed to the mystery of a faith that, although beyond words, requires our inadequate wording, the assembly praising God's creation as best as our eyes will allow.

Writing about any believer who is ignorant of astronomical science, Kepler wrote, "He should raise his eyes (his only means of vision) to this visible heaven and with his whole heart burst forth in giving thanks and praising God the Creator. He can be sure that he worships God no less than the astronomer, to whom God has granted the more penetrating vision of the mind's eye, and an ability and desire to celebrate his God above those things he has discovered."[11] May even the historic creeds take their place in carrying both our eyes and our minds in albeit limited praise to God.

17 *Chapter*

Praying the Intercessions
with Dorothy Day

Dorothy Day appears to me to have been something of an Amish Roman Catholic. Founder and editor of *The Catholic Worker*, Day was a wife, a partner, a mother, grandmother and great-grandmother; a nurse, journalist, novelist, libertarian; and an activist who, arrested eleven times, rendered endless support to the working poor, joined their picket lines, defended strikers, established Houses of Hospitality for the homeless, operated breadlines for the hungry, maintained voluntary poverty, challenged the church's hierarchy toward more courageous witness to Christ, praised the world's political revolutions, and incessantly spoke out against wealth inequalities, war, anti-Semitism, racial discrimination, sexual promiscuity, and the dehumanizing patterns of modern life. She died of heart failure on November 29, 1980—an apt conclusion to a life that, although characterized by profound joy, suffered from personal, communal, ecclesial, national, and international heartache. Has this introduction omitted anything that you most respect about Dorothy Day?

First, her Amish-like characteristics: Day was catechized and baptized in the Episcopal Church as a thirteen-year-old, but most accounts of her life make little or nothing of this sacramental event. Rather, as with the Anabaptists of the sixteenth century, the baptism that features in her narrative is her re-baptism, a product of the pre-ecumenical practices of the time, when at the age of twenty-nine she presented herself at the font to commence an adult life of faith and commitment. Like contemporary Amish Christians, she was an absolute pacifist, for both offensive and defensive war. Like most American Amish, she never voted at national elections. Her literal interpretation of the Sermon on the Mount—"The Sermon on the Mount answered all the questions as to how to love God and one's brother"[1]—as the primary rule of life would resonate with the Amish. Like the Amish, she maintained that cooperative living on small farms was the best way to nurture Christian values, writing as late as 1972, "We need communities of work, land for the landless, true farming communes. The heart hungers for that new social order wherein justice dwelleth."[2]

Now, to her Roman Catholic characteristics: For fifty years she maintained devout participation in the worship practices of the Roman Catholic Church, faithful to its daily Mass and its devotional rituals. She offered respect to that church's hierarchy. The metaphor so important in Roman Catholic theology—the Mystical Body of Christ, we being members of one another—was her spiritual center, grounding her own identity in that of the whole church, especially with its poor. She is honored by the Vatican with the title Servant of God. Pope Francis said when addressing a joint meeting of Congress in September 2015 that she is revered for "her passion for justice and for the cause of the oppressed."[3] What the Roman tradition calls "the corporal works of mercy," taken from Matthew 25:35-36—feeding the hungry, giving drink to the thirsty, clothing the naked, sheltering the homeless, visiting the sick, visiting the imprisoned, and burying the dead—was her to-do list. Her hopes for farming communes that gathered everyone for daily Eucharist were inspired by medieval monasteries. She was a supreme idealist within Roman Catholicism, a branch of Christianity already receptive to idealisms.

I honor Day for her endless search for social justice. However, given her notions of minimal government and the

preference of agrarian life, she seems to me a reactionary, maintaining ideals that Americans know from Thomas Jefferson. I
do not understand her disdain for government, since it did
come to provide some of the relief for the poor and the protection for workers that she sought. About farming communes,
she wrote in 1952, "The savings of those who do not smoke,
drink beer, go to movies, use cosmetics, buy radios, cars, television sets, should be enough to buy a farm to enable them to
make a start."[4] Was she serious? In defense of her commitment
to pacifism, she recorded that she and another woman were
able to gently wrest a bread knife away from a violent intruder.[5]
I cannot accept this anecdote as a worthy response to the Christian agony when confronted with the Third Reich. I see lots of
gray coloring her black-and-white world.

Yet for our purposes on Sunday, I urge us to remember that
she prayed, and prayed, and prayed. Her writings testify to
her dedication to continual prayer. It is reported that " 'to im-
portune' was one of Dorothy's signature phrases. People were
always importuning her, she said."[6] The biblical passage now
usually called "the parable of the unjust judge" was in earlier
decades titled "the parable of the importunate widow." Like
this widow in Luke 18, Day was always importuning God,
which is what the assembly's communal prayers intend. These
petitions are the primary location in the liturgy that give voice
to the innumerable sufferings of the world, the endless agonies
of the poor, the wrenching sorrows of our neighbors. Are we
giving sufficient attention to this aspect of our worship? Catherine of Siena prayed, "Give us a voice, your own voice, to cry
out to you for mercy for the world and for the reform of holy
Church."[7] I suggest that as we consider the content and tone
of the intercessions communally offered each Sunday, we become the voice of Christ, inspired by the ministry of Dorothy
Day, as if now she is importuning us to pray.

We can begin by reflecting on a small section of the General
Prayer that was provided a century ago for use at every service
of Holy Communion among one large grouping of American

Lutherans:[8] "All who are in trouble, want, sickness, anguish of labor, peril of death, or any other adversity, especially those who are in suffering for Thy Name and for Thy truth's sake, comfort, O God, with Thy Holy Spirit. . . . We entreat Thee, O most Merciful Father, out of Thine unspeakable goodness, grace and mercy, defend us from all harm and danger of body and soul. Preserve us from false and pernicious doctrine, from war and bloodshed, from plague and pestilence, from all calamity by fire and water, from hail and tempest, from failure of harvest and from famine, from anguish of heart and despair of Thy mercy, and from an evil death. And in every time of trouble, show Thyself a very present Help, the Saviour of all men, and especially of them that believe." These laden sentences are only part of a lengthy prayer that pleaded, among other things, for the church universal, faithful teaching of doctrine, mission work, the institutions of the church, seminarians, Christian homes, all in authority, the president and Congress, the governor, judges, and fruitful harvest. Despite the archaic prose, I like the line "Give success to all lawful occupations on land and sea; to all pure arts and useful knowledge; and crown them with Thy blessing." A rubric directs the addition of yet more "special supplications, intercessions and prayers" to grant timeliness to the prayer.

This breathtaking collection of petitions offers much for our consideration. It assumes that all people perpetually face troubles of every kind, and it appeals to the mighty God in the face of endless agonies. Do we want to cultivate such an attitude among worshipers on Sunday morning? The assembly does not wait until political disaster or calamitous weather brings suffering and destruction; rather, it begs in advance for safety. How ought we evaluate this approach to prayer? Our brief requests are shamed by the astounding inclusivity of these petitions, as each week the church, the home, the government, and the needy throughout the globe are listed in detail. Is such a weekly repetition a worthy goal, or merely a tedious enumeration? Would people glaze over and lose attention during such a prayer, or would its repetition allow worshipers to focus on one paragraph on one Sunday but another paragraph next Sunday? What has been gained, and what has been lost, in our current practice of short petitions crafted each week by each congregation, rather than the use of one substantial standard text?

Liturgical scholars suggest that early Christian communities included intercessions at their weekly meal meetings. Over the centuries, the intercessions dropped out, replaced by prayers that focused in the collect on the assembled believers and in the eucharistic prayer on the dead. The 1917 prayer cited above is one example of a church body urging the return to full weekly intercessions. Some Protestant churches have regularized the practice of the pastoral prayer, which is extemporized by the preacher after the sermon, to sum up whatever was the focus of the morning's Scripture. In the denominations that adopted the liturgical reforms of the twentieth century, the intercessions have returned, usually in litany form, either primed by publications disseminated by denominational publishing houses or crafted by the clergy or by trained local laypeople. What is your experience of these intercessions? Alas, I find that too often the intercessions are perhaps four tame—or lame—sentences. Many of these petitions are nonspecific enough to have been composed a decade ago, although perhaps one mentions a newsworthy item of human need.

I do not know how prayer functions. I am uncomfortable with the word "miracle," yet I trust that there is more to Christian prayer than communal consciousness raising or personal requests made public. I remain moved by the words of a young pastor who said to me that, whatever prayer is, she is called to the ministry of intercession. So I channel the "communitarian radical"[9] Dorothy Day.

It is customary to open the intercessions with prayers for the church. Day both honored and criticized the leadership of the church and the witness of the baptized. What does our prayer include as "the church"? What during this week cries out for our prayers? Which ecclesial leaders or other denominations need our prayers? How ought we word our petitions so that they name specifically the needs of the church, without becoming a bulletin board of upcoming scheduled events?

Recently, some churches have come to include a weekly petition for the earth, and not merely for healthy harvest, which would have been a regular concern for Day's farming communes. Day also wrote in delight about the dove in the mimosa tree at her Staten Island beach house as a sign of God's loving creation. What issues related to the effects of global climate change reach out for our prayers? What plants, which animals, are dying, for which we must beg God for a continuing creation? Is there local green space on which we ask God's blessing?

Next come the petitions for peace and justice. Decade by decade, Day was always writing about the horrors of war and the wrongheadedness of preparation for war. In the 1950s, she was arrested for refusing to participate in the civil defense drills held in New York City, and she urged believers to withhold income taxes that financed future war efforts. What ought to be our tasks as citizens of a nation filled with Christians, yet involved in perpetual warfare the world over? Ought our prayers list perhaps the three countries most afflicted by war during the past week? Remember that the journalist Day did not hide behind blah-blah-blah, but spoke in plain speech to the nation, to the church, and to God. Do we here pray for our enemies—whomever we consider them to be?

Perhaps Day's primary life focus was attention to the misery of the poor, both those underpaid and those unemployed. When she began her support of the pickets of labor unions, there was no minimum wage, no unemployment insurance, no benefits for the laboring masses, with this laissez-faire attitude of government supported by a widespread national sense that any labor collaboration was anti-Christian and communist-inspired. Her focus was ever alert, whether dealing with the conditions in the mines, or discrimination of African Americans, or the treatment of migrant farmworkers, or the prejudice against immigrants, or the imprisonment of draft resistors. Did anything happen over this past week that makes survival of the poor and the oppressed even harder than it was a month ago? How ought our weekly intercessions address the growing wealth inequity in society? Day hoped that communes of urban folk, if provided with land, could farm their own food, yet even she admitted that these farms did not achieve her noble aims.[10] How ought we, in a society moving past an agrarian economy, beyond the industrial age, and into the time of technology, be presenting the intensifying needs of the poor before the mercy of almighty God? And how can we ensure that such petitions are not heard as rules for our conduct, ordering what we must do during the coming week? How are our intercessions signposts of divine grace? As Day titled a set of her memoirs, "All is grace."[11]

Then comes our prayer for all who are in trouble, want, sickness, or other adversity. Who compiles and monitors this list? Please reflect with me on what is sometimes a lengthy list of names. How does this list function? Is this evidence of the human hope for magic, that if a name is called out up close to the altar, God will surely attend? Is such a list most meant for the assembly, as news bulletins about the local sick, or as reminder of the needs of our neighbors? How many names ought to be included? What about the issue of confidentiality? Does it matter that the persons named are not known to the assembly? For how many weeks should a name remain on the list?

And then there are all those other concerns: interchurch cooperation, parish catechesis, the protection of rhinos, a local election, jury duty, the police force, refugees, victims of sexual violence, persons in recovery, a new devastating virus. We think through Day's corporal works of mercy, and perhaps this week we add our care for prisoners. And should there be a space of silence as we each plead for the desires of our own hearts? How many minutes ought this prayer take?

As a Lutheran, I do not pray for the dead, already having given them into God's mercy. However, the final paragraph of the intercessions praises God for the lives of the faithful de-

parted, naming saints and the recently deceased, and I hope
that on the Sunday nearest to November 29, our list of the dead
will include Dorothy Day. Can we keep alive among us her
spirit of importuning for a world so full of need?

In 1969, Dorothy Day remarked, "Without prayer we could
not continue,"[12] and in 1970 wrote, "I have been overcome with
grief at times, and felt my heart like a stone in my breast, it
was so heavy, and always I have heard, too, that voice, 'Pray.'
What can we do? We can pray. We can pray without ceasing,
as St. Paul said. We can say with the Apostles, 'Lord, teach me
to pray.' "[13] Thank you, Dorothy Day, for your voice as we
shape Sunday worship.

18
Chapter

Presenting the Offerings with Lawrence

L awrence, born in Spain and martyred under Emperor Valerian in 258, was one of the seven deacons of the churches in Rome. Inspired by the account in Acts 6 of the men selected to follow Christ by serving the needs of the poor, deacons in the third century had not yet developed a uniform ministry. Yet deacons had acquired a variety of responsibilities, such as distributing food to the poor, assisting the bishop with pastoral care, and overseeing the possessions of the church, which at that time would have included the eucharistic vessels and liturgical copies of biblical books. It seems that the deacons' close attention to locals who were sick or hungry led to their being assigned the crafting of intercessions at the Sunday liturgy. Although as a Roman citizen Lawrence ought to have been granted execution by beheading, tradition says that he was tortured and then put to death on a grill. He is commemorated on August 10.

Of Lawrence are told two captivating stories: When ordered by the Roman prefect to relinquish to the state the contents of the church treasury, Lawrence asked for several days to complete the task. He used the time to sell what he could and to donate the money to the poor, and then at the appointed hour he presented to the officials a group of the church's poor—the widows, the maimed, the homeless, the wretched—and said, "These are the treasures of the church." And when he was convicted and roasting on a grill, his last words were, "Turn me over, I'm done on that side."

May we all enrich our lives with such care for the poor, and may we all await our death with the spirit of Lawrence.

I hear Lawrence saying only one thing to us about Sunday worship: quite simply, that every single celebration of Holy Communion include a ritually significant collection for the poor. I am thinking not merely about a gentle reminder about our obligations for the needy, nor of updates on the clothing drive. Nor ought we rely on the writings of Luke or Paul to handle this touchy subject. Rather, we need to remember, and liturgically to enact, that we partake in the Eucharist not only for ourselves, but are in the meal bound to all who suffer, all who sorrow, all in misery. Our attention is directed not only to the wounds of Christ, but also to all the wounded around the earth.

In Christianity, the way worshipers offer a gift to God is to give to the needy. In one Baptist church I know, the whole assembly processes up to the altar to place their contributions into baskets. I do understand the budgetary advantage for congregations to urge members to arrange that their contributions be sent from their bank account by direct deposit to the church office. Yet when this is the case, we can also urge worshipers to place at least a dollar in the plate as a sign that our reception of divine mercy impels us to give to others. Is it made clear to members where the money from the collection is headed? (Perhaps the bill for resurfacing the church's parking lot ought not be covered by the funds collected for the poor.) At what age do children begin receiving a weekly allowance? I hope those very young Christians are already being taught to tithe their dollar a week with the dime they put into the plate.

In those churches in which the bread and wine are brought up to the altar at this time, how are these elements connected in any genuine way with the assembly's gifts of food for the hungry?

In his personal conclusion to the letter to the Romans, Paul wrote, "I commend to you our sister Phoebe, a deacon of the church at Cenchreae, so that you may welcome her in the Lord as is fitting for the saints, and help her in whatever she may require from you, for she has been a benefactor of many and of myself as well" (16:1-2). Deacons both, Phoebe and Lawrence lived as benefactors of mercy. And we join them, every Sunday.

Chapter 19

Passing the Peace with Francis of Assisi

Perhaps the most indisputable way that Francis of Assisi resembled Jesus of Nazareth is that the precise facts of their biographies are beyond retrieval. Was Jesus really born in Bethlehem? Did Francis actually preach to birds? Did Jesus change water into wine? According to the life of Francis as written by Bonaventure, Francis also performed this miracle.[1] Did Jesus walk on water—or was the story a metaphor to proclaim the divinity of Christ? Did Francis's hand shake the paw of the wolf of Gubbio—or did the story mean to liken the wolf to the predatory upper classes, who were dreaded for their practices of stealing from the poor? Which biblical account of Christ's resurrection do you most value? Which description of the wounds on Francis's body do you credit?

In striking parallel with the search for the historical Jesus begun in the nineteenth century, recent biographies of Francis, of which there are a goodly number, dedicate much text and extensive notes to suggest which were the genuine adventures of Francis. Biographers distinguish between what they judge to be historically accurate accounts that were recorded during Francis's life or soon after his death on October 4, 1226, from what were later theological interpretations of memories, or indeed wholly unreliable hagiographic tropes, accepted by medieval Christians as proofs of sanctity.[2] Readers encounter lots of the subjunctive mood and the adverb "probably" in these biographies. Scholars give credence to one paragraph of some source, but dismiss the facticity of the following paragraph. It is something of a muddle. The authors theorize why over time some tales became beloved legends, as each decade, each century, including our own time, tells the story of Francis in its own categories, for its own purposes. I am not exempt: here is my view of Francis, for the purpose of improving Sunday worship.

It is said that Francis greeted everyone with the words, "May the Lord give you peace," and this during a century marked by indescribable butchery on the battlefields, vindictiveness among church leaders, deceit within the local community, and even alienation within Francis's own family. In our time people all around the world are accustomed to wishing one another peace, even using an identical gesture of raising up their fingers as a V. In contrast, historians write that in the thirteenth century, such a salutation—a friendly greeting exchanged between strangers—would have sounded idiosyncratic, even bizarre. Here let me discuss four examples from history and legend of Francis's expressions of peace:

Francis was always turned toward the poor, and repeatedly throughout his life, it was the lepers, living in wretched conditions, whom Francis served. Rather than running away from the warning rattles of approaching lepers, he went toward them, greeting them with peace, binding their wounds, offering them food, attending to their needs. In his Italy, lepers represented the absolute other, the beings wholly outside the pale, from whom infirmity and death were contagious. By turning away from the well-dressed clientele of his father's successful import business and toward the ragged lepers, Francis demonstrated a welcome to the other that distressed his family, shocked his contemporaries, and humbles us still today. For Francis, who knew his Matthew 25, these despised brothers and sisters were Christ, and so he embraced them with peace.

Although most biographies of Francis deal with the stigmata as a heaven-sent replication of the wounds of the crucified Christ onto Francis's body,[3] I am drawn to the suggestion that these lesions borne by Francis were perhaps the ravages of leprosy, a disease he likely had contracted from his decades of serving these diseased poor.[4] By deconstructing the story of the stigmata, we can liken Francis to the apostle Paul, writing in Galatians 6:17 that he was branded with the marks of Jesus, the wreck of his body the result of a life that had walked the way of the cross. To me, such an interpretation of Francis's wounds connects him more profoundly with Jesus Christ than would some miraculous reiteration of Calvary.

A second example from the stories of Francis is the memory of his preaching to the birds. He seems to have had a remarkable affinity for animals, with later legends including the charming tale of his taming the wolf. Although the animals are among the other in God's creation, Francis shared God's peace with them.

A third example: To our wonderment, in September 1219, during the disastrous Fifth Crusade, Francis—already in pitiable physical condition suffering from, among other ailments, recurring malaria, an acute gastric ulcer, an enlarged liver, and possibly already the agonizingly painful trachoma of his last years—got himself over to Damietta, Egypt, to attempt to convert Sultan al-Malik al-Kamil to Christianity. (Or was Francis's intention to achieve martyrdom?) Also in this extraordinary adventure, Francis embraced the other. The Sultan as a Muslim was usually demonized by the Christian world, and yet Francis saw him through the light of the peace of Christ.

At the last, more dead than alive and far beyond thirteenth-century medicine, Francis dictated his final stanza to his Canticle:[5]

> All praise be yours, my Lord, through Sister Death,
>   from whose embrace no mortal can escape.
> Happy those she finds doing your will!
> Praise and bless my Lord, and give him thanks,
>   and serve him with great humility.

And although St. Paul wrote of death as the last enemy that Christ will destroy, Francis died welcoming the final other, death itself, as a sister provided by God.

So this is Francis: welcoming the other—the lepers, the animals, the sultan, even death—while extending the peace of the Lord to all. Now to Sunday morning.

In five places in the New Testament, Christians are reminded to greet one another with a holy kiss. In that first-century society, a full kiss, mouth to mouth, was normally reserved for the nuclear family and lovers, and was conducted in private. By incorporating this ritual in their weekly meetings, Christian assemblies meant to establish their community as a fictive family, a bounded religious community that in some ways replaced their natural family. This kiss was unusual—it was "holy," whatever that meant—and unconventional—a private sign made public. By the third century, bishops claimed the right to offer the first holy kiss to the newly baptized, who would not have participated in this ritual of faith before their initiation. By the thirteenth century, any physical contact had been replaced by the passing of the pax board, a tablet on which was a depiction of Christ. (One certainly does wonder what had been going on to incite this liturgical malformation in assemblies where the sexes stood separated from one another.) By the sixteenth century, although in some churches the presider extended Christ's peace orally to the assembly, no communal ritual of the holy kiss was retained.[6]

Following the lead of the Church of South India in 1950, many churches in the late twentieth century revived the holy kiss, albeit in the culturally acceptable form of a handshake, an embrace, or a bow. Are you old enough to remember the intensity of resistance during the 1960s to this enculturation of ancient practice? We smile at the anecdote of the elderly lady busy at Mass saying her rosary and, at the newly instituted sign of peace, responding to her neighbor, "I don't believe in that shit."[7] (Ah, elderly ladies!) In my earliest experience, the passing of the peace was clericalized: the handclasp was initiated between the presider and a vested assistant, and then was passed down the aisle and along each pew until everyone had received from one person and given to one other a handshake.

Currently, in some churches, especially among Protestants who pass the peace after the proclamation of the Word, the ritual has become a kind of seventh-inning stretch, with folks rushing around the nave, giving a quick hello to as many persons as they can, Peace here, Peace there, sometimes not taking time for eye contact, in such a hurry they are, looking for whom else to greet. Such cheery interactions—"Did you remember to bring the cookies for coffee hour?"—can dissipate whatever aura of religious intensity had been established by the proclamation and exposition of the Word. I have found that saying the full sentence "May the peace of the risen Christ be with you" does slow things down a bit. Perhaps among Roman Catholics, who pass the peace just prior to communing, the peace is more staid. However, some churches, acknowledging that in their situation the ritual is genuinely merely a friendly salutation, place this ritual during the opening rites of greeting. (What do you think of that?)

If decades ago people had been taught that this peace is the greeting of the risen Christ on Easter evening, not merely a sign of fellowship, but rather a profoundly spiritual sharing of the power of the Holy Spirit, this seems to have been forgotten. (Such catechesis about the meaning of the liturgical peace needs to be repeated annually—perhaps on the second Sunday of Easter.) Too often during our worship, the handshake is passed only among family members or from friend to friend without being extended to those whom we do not know or with whom we are quarreling. Although I am grateful for this ritual, a gesture that invites the baptized to greet one another in peace in recognition that the individual is not worshiping alone, we must admit that our use of a familiar and informal handshake has substituted a customary social greeting, as tame as can be, for what was a startling faith claim in the early church, that the other was now sister and brother.

A perfunctory handshake stands far indeed from Francis's disconcerting embrace of the other. Often there is little of the resurrection and nothing of other in the gesture. I wish that receiving and passing the peace of Christ could regain some of its wonder, that we stand stunned to share with one another our faith in the resurrection, each person admitting that even between friendly members of the Sunday assembly a great gulf is fixed, recognizing and honoring the mysterious distance between the self and the others. We welcome the other, but we cannot become the other, and only the peace of Christ bridges the chasm.

As Francis said when first designing a Rule for his emerging order, "Let any brother who desires go among the Saracens and other nonbelievers. . . . Wherever they may be, let all my brothers remember that they have given themselves and abandoned their bodies to the Lord Jesus Christ. For love of him, they must make themselves vulnerable to their enemies."[8] Note the word "enemies." Francis did not sentimentalize the greeting between ourselves and others. Yet we greet these others, and share with them the peace of Christ, making ourselves vulnerable to them. Although many communicants worry about catching the common cold, or something rather worse, from their drinking from the common cup, it is in fact in shaking one another's hand—that is, in passing the peace—that we participate in the greatest possibility of contagion. Our hands, not brandishing a weapon, but held open, palms exposed, are by this ritual open to all the microbes of family, friend, stranger, and enemy, the simple handshake a sign of our vulnerability to the other—so less superficial a gesture than we might have thought.

One place that each year the assembly prays for the other is in Good Friday's bidding prayer. As we gather around the foot of the cross, our prayer for everything and everybody in the world is structured of concentric circles, each circle farther away from our small center. First is a petition for the whole church, then the clergy and the leaders of the church, then those preparing for baptism, then all the people who share our faith. But then we come to the other, as we offer petitions for the Jews, for members of other religions, and for those who do not subscribe to any religion at all. How are we to word these prayers? Are we to remain aware of the distance between us and these others? Or there at Golgotha are we to gather all the others to our assembly? In either case, along with Francis, we approach the other in respect and for service.

Francis welcomed even Sister Death. In a retirement home is a poster advertising a seminar on "Aging Backwards": alas, for many this means going back to the helplessness of infancy, in a time when medical care can keep us alive, and keep us alive, and keep us alive. I have long taught that Sunday worship is practice for dying—especially necessary in a culture in which people avoid even pronouncing the word "die," although I have not yet heard anyone say that Jesus "passed." He died, and so will we, and perhaps also you know old and sick Christians pleading for the arrival of Sister Death. So how ought the worshiping community prepare for death? Somewhere in our worship space will be a crucifix, for we gather always at the foot of the dying Christ. We trace on our bodies the sign of that cross, as if already today giving our body over to the care of Sister Death. Each week, we remember the faithful departed, either in gratitude or supplication. Our ethical reflections will know ourselves to be, not little deities running around with self-appointed power, but mortal creatures, born, alive, and finally dead, all through the mercy of God, in whom alone resides eternal life.

"May the Lord give you peace," said the follower of Christ. May the passing of the peace in our assemblies become all that it intends.

Chapter 20

Fostering Ecumenism with Brother Roger

R oger Schütz-Marsauche spent his life fostering reconciliation among churches, nations, and individuals, as
well as between ourselves and God. Born in 1915, in
1940 he appropriated use of a house in Taizé, a small village
near Cluny, France, for the purpose of protecting and assisting
war refugees, especially Jews. By 1949, six men had joined
him in vows to establish the Taizé Community, unique in the
world at that time as an ecumenical monastery. The brothers
in the community, although coming from various denominations, were to be united in prayerful living, in solidarity with
all who suffer, "called to live the parable of community."[1] Taizé
began to attract an increasing number of visitors, which led
to the building of the monastery's huge worship space, the
construction of which was assisted by German youths after
World War II as their own act of reconciliation to France. The
community's discipline of daily prayer effected a unity of
Christians that is other than that of ecclesial institutions and
doctrinal agreements. Known now as Brother Roger, he was
a beloved international emissary of the ecumenical movement,
joining in prayer with leaders and laity of Roman Catholicism,
Orthodoxy, and Protestantism, carrying himself around the
world as a sign of the communion of churches and inspiring
others to pray as one in the Body of Christ. This man of reconciliation died on August 16, 2005, from a violent attack
while he was with the community at prayer in Taizé's own
Church of Reconciliation.

Brother Roger gradually laid down prerogatives of his Swiss Protestant clerical ordination so that, although prior of his community, he could be one with his brothers. He oversaw the original Rule and the later development of the Taizé Community, which now has about a hundred brothers. Always some of the brothers live away from Taizé in places around the globe of extreme poverty and political tension, their presence a sign of reconciliation across barriers of economic disparity, national interests, and religious differences. Beginning in 1966, the brothers were instrumental in establishing the international youth gatherings. Continuing this ministry of reconciliation, Taizé has become the world's most important Christian youth retreat center, visited by up to six thousand young people each week. "Taizé is not a home, a refuge, a shelter, a sect. It is simply a place of pilgrimage. Pilgrims come, are refreshed, and move on."[2] Yes, they move on—having been transformed by the practice of ecumenical worship. "Faith was discovered as a communal reality and not simply a subjective experience."[3]

Brother Roger's commitment to ecumenical reconciliation is evident in the text of the first Rule he wrote for the brothers: "Never resign yourself to the scandal of the separation of Christians, all so readily professing love for their neighbor, yet remaining divided. Make the unity of Christ's Body your passionate concern."[4] Under the guidance of Brother Roger, the liturgical life at Taizé came to include rituals from all the major branches of Christianity: reliance on the Roman Catholic practice of *lectio divina*, in which Scripture readings are followed by substantial periods of meditation; from Eastern Orthodox spirituality, plentiful use of icons and candles; from the Reformation churches, assembly singing of biblical texts; and from the Anglican Communion, the practice of Protestant monasticism. Brother Roger believed that by praying together, Christians will come to a fuller communion of the churches: worship in common could precede, as well as follow upon, formal ecumenical agreements. To describe how the branches of Christianity need one another, he wrote, "In the southern languages the word for Church means meeting or—even better—assembly: *ecclesia, église, iglesia, chiesa*. In northern languages the Church is designated by the name of the Lord (*Kyrios*): church, *Kirche, kyrka,* kerk. So there too south and north complement one another."[5] He spoke of his hope that the churches could reconcile without recriminations, without any Christians having to regret or renounce their own family of believers as they bring into reality their communion with one another.

And now to our Sundays and to my hope that without making a retreat at Taizé, we all can foster ecumenism as we worship.

I do not intend by this attention to ecumenism to lend support to the idealistic hope that some original unity of the church must be restored,[6] as if, in penning John 17, the Johannine community is instructing Protestants and Orthodox to return to Rome. Indeed, the New Testament indicates that also the earliest Christians were separated into factions. I do not imagine, nor even desire, a single Christian organization on earth, and I am each week grateful for the Lutheran heritage alive and well in my congregation. (Let's get real: by the second day of any such worldwide union of the baptized, some assembly would break itself off, the better to realize one particular belief or goal.) Indeed, some sociologists suggest that one way to account for the higher church attendance in the United States than in Europe is because of the accessibility of different denominations: a family is disgusted by some nonsense in church A, and so they head down the block to church B. While visiting other churches, I have come to admire their denominationally distinctive rituals—that at Christian Love Baptist Church, a long introductory time of communal song unites the worshipers into one assembly; that Roman Catholics do not require ushers to escort the people up for Communion; that Mennonites sing one hymn after another in four-part harmony; that the Seventh-Day Adventists conduct a foot-washing quarterly with no apparent emotional shenanigans—although I can't think how to emulate Easter Day at St. John the Divine in New York City, when an elephant and an ostrich join in the opening procession.

My hope for ecumenism recalls Paul in Galatians 2, reporting that the reconciliation between himself and Peter after the controversy about Gentile membership was ritualized with "the right hand of fellowship," and not by appointing some single overarching authority. Yet I do pray for a strengthening of the communion of churches. The French philosopher Hélène Cixous, when discussing feminism, offered a startling response to the perennial question "Who am I?" Wrong question, she said: the better question is "Who are I?"[7] We are already part of one another, and for the health of each, we must rejoice in and strengthen that connection, and we can do so at Sunday worship.

I visited Taizé many years ago—before the rows of tents, before the sanctuary's signature orange sails.[8] The way I best know the ministry of Brother Roger is the same way that much of the Christian world does: through the music of Jacques Berthier. The brothers discovered that the pilgrims, gathered from many countries, speaking their own languages, could not genuinely participate in prayer chanted in French. Worship in common needed some creative musical and linguistic innovation: any single ecclesial tradition offered little help here. The choice of Berthier in 1974 to provide a solution has become a gift for us all.[9] Especially his ostinato form is itself a symbol of the communion of churches: the assembly repeats a simple biblical phrase to an accessible musical line, while instrumentalists, soloists, or a choir enhance the song with overlays of words and tune. Into one song is both unity and diversity—or as Brother Roger titled one of his books, "unanimity in pluralism": both need the other. And which language should gain precedence? In some of Berthier's songs, Latin—nobody's language, and its syllables are easy to pronounce—is used. In others, each language takes its turn.

Many of us need go only as far as our parish church to discover something of an ecumenical assembly. Yes, there remain congregations that are remarkably homogenous in history, doctrine, language, and style. There are, for example, the Amish. (Perhaps half a dozen other such denominations are still around.) But increasingly, at least in the northern hemisphere, Sunday morning assemblies are heterogenous, their members speaking several different languages and preferring varied styles of music and manner. The assembly, the musicians, even the clergy have come together from various denominations, and they bring with them on Sunday morning—at least in their memory—an alternate way, a part that offers value to the whole. Let me suggest some ways that in each of the many churches, the whole of the church can be honored and ecumenism fostered.

Some churches have replaced their historic terminology with the language of the ecumenical *ordo*. We gather, we receive the Word, we share the meal, and are sent out for service. On the deepest level, our worship as Christians is a shared pattern.

The two versions of the three-year ecumenical lectionary—the Roman Lectionary and the Revised Common Lectionary—are a treasure chest filled with the word of God, one gem upon another, glistening with life from the Spirit, and publishing houses sponsored by Roman Catholics and Protestants are providing a wealth of biblical aids and parish resources to interpret and embody the texts. Thus, we can now be one at least in the Word. (Do your people all know this?) In some localities, those who preach regularly meet for interdenominational lectionary study, each church sharing with others, each community learning from others.

Churches are no longer routinely administering a second baptism to newcomers who have already been baptized in some other church.

That Sunday is the primary day for the celebration of Holy Communion is a growing ecumenical understanding.

We can join Christians around the globe in singing Berthier's chants, especially his ostinato form, particularly when walking up and down the aisles during the Communion.

Our ubiquitous service folders might foster ecumenism. Perhaps where a hymn is cited, the ecclesial traditions of the author and of the composer might be listed: the hymn text written by Ambrose, or by an old-time Methodist, or by a nun in Minnesota, and the tune from the Middle Ages, or the German Reformation, or the shape-note song of Appalachian farmers. Such information would demonstrate that our liturgical corpus is already ecumenical.

In those churches that commemorate the faithful departed, lists no longer serve merely as denominational histories, but as invitations to thank God for all the baptized who have gone before us. If we print their biographical sketches in the service folder, we can be sure to mention the denomination that nurtured their faith.

Admittedly, some ecumenical liturgical practices do not appear in our assemblies with minimal notice but, rather like the controversy between Peter and Paul, can cause considerable commotion, even pained dismay. Religious ritual is essentially conservative, but the complication to this truism about religion is that in Christianity, the dead are raised to new life, and everything can become new. Thus the human instinct for the community to repeat last year's ritual hears the call to walk away from the empty tomb with one another on paths as yet untrodden.

An example of this startling newness is the translations of common liturgical texts. In the last decades of the twentieth century, before lower church attendance lured many congregations into caring solely about themselves, ecumenical committees supported by national church offices struggled word by word through the classic liturgical texts to offer a shared ecumenical English translation.[10] Some of these texts have been readily accepted: composers now set to music "Lord, God of power and might," not "of Sabaoth," thus replacing that easily misunderstood Hebrew word with some of its meaning. But not all ecumenical translations have made the denominational cut: may it be that once again English-speaking Christians can greet others with the words "The Lord be with you" and receive a resounding unison response.

The ecumenical text of the Lord's Prayer seems to be slowest in occupying our minds and hearts. Proposed first in 1975 (thus, hardly a "new" translation), the translation of the Our Father offered by the Consultation on Common Texts is praised by New Testament scholars as more accurate to the biblical text than that of earlier centuries. Worshipers will no longer assume that the pronouns "thy" and "thine" indicate how elevated and distant is God, when actually—Quaker style—those pronouns, in the seventeenth century, addressed both God and one's nearest and dearest with the identical terms of intimacy. The petition "save us from the time of trial" relieves us of the need to teach against the earlier wording "lead us not into temptation," which is recognized by theologians as a highly misleading phrase. Now we can thank God for a better translation, joining with English speakers around the world to pray more biblically. The obvious question for each assembly is: ought our prayer in the Sunday assembly befit those believers who resist adopting a new translation, or ought our prayer shape the faith of the neophytes, more scripturally, more ecumenically?

One characteristic of Taizé worship that may be profoundly effective for young pilgrims but problematic for communal worship is its cultivated periods of contemplative silence. Some silence on Sunday, yes. But with infants, toddlers, and preschoolers present, lengthy meditation? I'd say no.

In a letter in 2005 Brother Roger wrote, "Will we do all we can for Christians to wake up to the spirit of communion? 'Communion' is one of the most beautiful names of the church."[11] In ways either small or momentous, our Sunday worship can receive and express the Spirit of communion, not only with the risen Christ, not only with our own assembly, but also with churches like ours and not like ours, all around the globe.

Chapter 21

Praising and Thanking with Thomas Cranmer

Thomas Cranmer, born in 1489, was always between. His biography shows a life always seeking for his rightful place between two opposites: the popes on one side, and the kings on the other; Henry VIII as a supportive intellectual companion, and Henry as an uncontrolled selfish tyrant; Queen Catherine of Aragon, and Queen Anne Boleyn; the law of clerical celibacy, and his loving commitment to his wife Margaret; his belief in the scriptural warrant for royal supremacy, versus the reality of unscrupulous court politics; the dictates of the curia, versus the reasoning of the new university professors; the people's medieval trust in miracles, versus his own attraction to the natural science of the Renaissance; classic Latin theology on one side, and the competing sixteenth-century European evangelical proposals on the other; the Western doctrine of transubstantiation, or Zwingli's teaching of the transformation of the heart; and about the succession, Henry's last will and testament in Mary's favor, versus Edward VI's dying choice of Jane Grey. Always he was between his personal preferences and his professional obligations. He supported the dissemination of a vernacular Bible, yet he was concerned over ignorant lay interpretations of it. He spent his final years in submission to Queen Mary, albeit suffering under her spirit of vindictiveness.

As the chief planner, compiler, editor, translator, and author of the *Book of Common Prayer*, Cranmer produced a religious masterpiece despite the tugs-of-war conducted by the two virulently oppositional camps within the Church of England. His ability to mediate these battles can be seen in the famous/infamous Black Rubric, which although he did not write, still expressed his view, according to which kneeling while receiving Communion was an act of gratitude and humility at the benefits that Christ afforded, but not of adoration of a divinized host. He kept his personal counsel on many issues, yet we can imagine his perpetual struggle between contraries in which he tended to see at least some truth on both sides. I am moved that although Thomas More opposed Cranmer's religious reforms, it came to be that when Henry VIII imprisoned More for refusing to acknowledge the king as the supreme head of the church, in pastoral compassion Cranmer ministered to Thomas More, urging him to find some way to escape execution.

Even on March 21, 1556, up on the scaffold, attired in a ragged gown, he stood between the recantations he had signed while importuned in prison and the enduring evangelical convictions of his heart. And while readers of this essay include descendants of both his Roman Catholic formation and his Protestant reforms, I trust that we are all grateful that Catholics are no longer burning Protestants, or Protestants burning Catholics, or both of them burning Anabaptists and whomever. At least when in 1536 William Tyndale was burned at the stake for having translated the Bible into English from the Hebrew and Greek rather than from the Latin Vulgate—some church history is nearly unbelievable—they mercifully strangled him first. No such kindness was granted to Thomas Cranmer. But had he been dead prior to the fire, he would not have been able to enact the awe-inspiring witness of his final confession of faith: while imprisoned, he had recanted his Protestant reforms, but at his execution he recanted that recantation, and thrust first into the fire his right hand with which he had signed the recantations that had been pressured on him by the crown.

In keeping with a life between, Cranmer perfected the authorial skill that characterizes the memorable rhetoric of the *Book of Common Prayer*, which thanks to the worldwide dissemination of this liturgical text throughout the British Empire, has helped to shape the English language in subsequent centuries. Of his twenty-four original collects, his primary biographer wrote, "These jeweled miniatures are one of the chief glories of the Anglican liturgical tradition."[1] In these collects, and in many other of his liturgical texts, it is his doublets that captivate me. Always there are two, A and B, and neither is enough without the other; each nuances the other; and the worshiper stands (or kneels?) between the two, almost levitating in the air. It is as if the liturgy acknowledges that the things of God lie beyond the capabilities of human speech. There must always be two— two nouns, two verbs, two adjectives. Yet there must be no excessive, empty jabber: as Cranmer wrote to Henry VIII about some changes that the king had proposed to a theological text of 1537, "I cannot perceive any manner of consideration why those words should be put in that place" and "This obscureth the sentence, and is superfluous."[2] (May all editors quote these sentences until the end of time.) So here is our task: how to emulate Cranmer's doublets, without superfluity.

Relying on doublets, Cranmer described his understanding of the presence of Christ in the Eucharist with these words: "I do as plainly speak as I can, that Christ's body and blood be given to us in deed, yet not corporally and carnally, but spiritually and effectually."[3] He needs doublets to speak plainly. In his masterpiece for the first Sunday of Lent, prayed by many of us on Ash Wednesday, God is everlasting and almighty (note, these are not synonyms); God hates nothing and forgives sins, creates and makes new and contrite hearts, as we lament our sins and acknowledge our wretchedness, and obtain remission and forgiveness.[4] Each doublet suggests one side of the mystery, and then we cross over the space to rest on the other side. In a collect for the second Sunday after Easter, Christ is given both as a sacrifice for sin and an example of godly life, and we are most thankfully to receive his benefits and daily endeavor ourselves to follow him.[5] That is, we both receive and follow, take and give. The doublets provide us space for praying, and this week, we can focus on one truth, next week on the other. In his prayer after Communion, "this our Sacrifice of praise and thanksgiving . . . this our bounden duty and service," he prays for grace and benediction, "not weighing our merits, but pardoning our offenses":[6] one doublet after another.

The last fifty years have witnessed the creation of absolute stacks of eucharistic prayers, disseminated by every technology from the sickly blue of Ditto machines to our own digital email. It is an exercise in humility to reread these liturgical attempts, many of us trying to express the mystery of God and the wonderment of the sacrament in phrasing both accessible and memorable, both theological and existential. We were both praising—that is, announcing to the world the marvels of creation and salvation—and thanking—that is, expressing gratitude for this meal and its mercies. (For to praise and to thank are not synonymous.) In the mid-twentieth century, convinced that American English was brusque and tight rather than weighty and labyrinthian, Hemingway better than Faulkner, what with worshipers stealing a glance at their watches (let's get down to coffee hour), many of us forgot Cranmer's doublets. Thus, many of our sentences were too thin to stand up on their own; they flopped right over. At least with doublets, there is a place to position both feet. Now, with a more mature and religiously weighted contemporary English, some doublets have returned: "O God most majestic, O God most motherly"[7] is a line in one eucharistic prayer, encouraging us first to kneel before the spectacular throne of the Almighty and then to rest in the comforting lap of our nursing mother. Alone, neither one is true enough. We need somehow to say both: bread and body, wine and blood, human and divine.

Here is a doublet: our Father in heaven. Father, the commonplace word we know from earliest childhood, is paired with heaven, the divine otherness beyond. I often hear extemporized prayers begin "Good and gracious God." That's fine, but these adjectives are more or less synonyms. We can continue to use the traditional doublets "almighty and merciful," might and mercy being two different qualities worthy of our praise and thanks. Sometimes the doublets can be expressed with the combination of an adjective and a noun—such as compassionate judge, sovereign lover, welcoming fire.

One liturgical doublet that Cranmer did not advocate is the widespread practice in our time of the assembly's singing of the *Sanctus* together with *Benedictus* as part of the eucharistic prayer. This liturgical song is the doublet form at its most consummate. For here we are, standing in our pews or at our chairs, or perhaps encircling the table. It's a standard Sunday, just us, with our usual vestments and paraments, and the vessels we like or don't like, and our adequate or inadequate versions of bread and wine, and our beloved or not-so-beloved presider. But in the first half of this chant, we are suddenly transformed into the nine ranks of angels around the throne of God, singing the endless "Holy, Holy, Holy." We are with Isaiah, in the sky-temple, and we are the chorus that the seer John hears singing to us from the end of time. And now, given our new ecological sensibilities, we realize that not only heaven, but also all of the earth is full of God's glory. (Goodness, what all does that mean?) The musical setting had better be worthy enough to express each of these divine domains.

But now, with the second half of the doublet, the scene shifts. In thinking about "Hosanna," we need to disregard our memories of Fauré's "The Palms," that joyously pompous nineteenth-century operatic choir anthem for Palm Sunday. For "Hosanna" does not mean exuberant praise praise praise. It means quite other: O God, save us. For we are now in the crowd of the poor on the streets of Jerusalem, pleading, even begging, for the Messiah to bring in the kingdom. You, Christ, are coming in the name of God, in the power of our Lord Most High. You, on that donkey, are God among us. So there on our table—or is it an altar? another doublet—is the presence of the God of heaven and earth, and there is also the body of Jesus, then in Jerusalem and here now in the bread.

The Swedish Lutheran composer and pastor Per Harling, in his version of the *Sanctus*, plays with the two words "holy" and "whole," originally the same word, which however by now have unrelated meanings: "You are holy, you are wholeness."[8] And another doublet: "You are always ever more than we ever understand, You are always at hand." We need to sing such texts repeatedly so as to be able to enter into each of the opposites and to balance ourselves between them. You can't rush through doublets of praise and thanks.

In the 1987 British film *A Month in the Country*, a young soldier, psychologically wounded from his service in the trenches of World War I, is spending the summer in a Yorkshire village church, restoring a fifteenth-century wall painting of the Final Judgment. The film—which is required viewing for everyone who cares about religious symbolism—opens with scenes of his crawling through the mud of the French battlefield, dragging himself under the barbed wire—and the background music is Franz Schubert's *Sanctus*. The filmmaker knew about doublets: the profound musical rendition of the "Holy, Holy, Holy," sung in German, accompanies the action of the German slaughter of the English. And then, having heard this superb liturgical chorus, we head off with the art restorer to witness the sadly barren worship conducted in that small Anglican church. The wall painting of the Final Judgment is of course also a doublet, the saved and the damned, both under Christ.

Even at home, as we pray before meals, Thomas Cranmer offers us doublets: "O Lord Jesus Christ, without whom nothing is sweet or savory; we beseech thee to bless us and our supper, and with thy blessed presence to cheer our hearts, that in all our meats and drinks, we may taste and savour of thee, to thy honour and glory."[9] Sweet or savory, bless us and cheer our hearts, our meats and drinks, taste and savour of thee, to thy honor and glory: God's honor, that is, what is in God we respect, and God's glory, that is, what radiates out from God to us. As Cranmer's doublets suggest, we eat both of our food and our God. I trust that at least on some occasions, we are not in too much of a hurry to praise and thank with such doublets.

Chapter 22

Greening Our Communion with Hildegard

Although virtually ignored for more than eight centuries while Western theologians were studying their patriarchal past, Hildegard of Bingen is once again speaking to the church. Born in 1098, she often suffered from illness, which probably included perennial migraines, while experiencing visions since the age of three. She was a child oblate, a professed Benedictine nun, the elected magistra of her community, the founder of two abbeys, and in old age a self-appointed traveling apocalyptic preacher. Encouraged by Pope Eugenius III, she composed three substantive works of visionary theology, sermons, gospel commentaries, liturgical poetry, two works of hagiography, and a morality play, with nearly four hundred letters extant. She fiercely excoriated those clergy whom she judged immoral or irresponsible. Most scholars agree that she also composed liturgical music and oversaw a striking set of manuscript illuminations. Inexplicable to scholars is the language of nine hundred words that she invented. She died in 1179 and is commemorated in several contemporary church calendars on her death day, September 17. Although not yet canonized in the Roman Catholic Church, Pope Benedict XVI honored her in 2012 with the title Doctor of the Church.

At times Hildegard dressed her nuns in floor-length white silk veils and idiosyncratic crowns of gold filigree adorned with symbols of the Trinity, defending this bizarre practice by claiming that as vowed virgins they in some way already celebrated the joys of paradise.[1] At several significant junctures, when her plans were thwarted by male authority figures, she experienced frightening bouts of paralysis, which were apparently effective in moving things along in the direction she desired. She insisted that the "living light" of the Holy Spirit was speaking through her and in this way deflected any medieval criticism that as a woman she could garner no authority. She was, however, something of a theological reactionary, maintaining classic Western views of male dominance, defending the social hierarchy that as a daughter of the nobility she enjoyed, approving Bernard of Clairvaux's support of the Crusades, and criticizing the emerging power of university scholasticism. Hildegard was a fierce spokesperson for her own views of faith and life, and her words are now back in print, albeit some in questionable translations and commandeered for causes that would have horrified her.[2]

What I suggest prods us on Sunday morning are her remarkable words about natural science. Along with most of her contemporaries, she believed that God had created a paradise for humankind, that nature was given to us humans for our benefit—see Genesis 1:28-29—and that infirmity and disease had resulted from the fall. But distinctive in the twelfth century was her insistence that her visions intended to teach humans as much as possible about the plants and animals God had created so that nature could be used for bodily healing. We marvel at her *Physica* and *Causae et Curae,* works of cosmology, botany, zoology, and holistic medicine that anthologize contemporaneous scientific data and to which it appears she added her own experience in the healing arts. Some of her advice sounds like our own: one ought to boil swamp water before drinking it. Some sounds like medieval folklore: powdered salmon bones are a remedy for rotting gums. One of my favorites is her suggestion that a bat, knocked senseless, tied to the loins of a human and left to die, is guaranteed to cure jaundice.[3] (Let's not fantasize about some gloriously wholesome past—"before penicillin and flush toilets," as an elderly friend of mine says.) Fascinating are her surprisingly accurate details relating to all aspects of human sexuality.

Her primary category when describing God's gift of the life force in nature was *viriditas,* which is usually translated "greenness," but in various contexts is rendered as freshness, vitality, greenery, fecundity, fruitfulness, verdure, or growth.[4] (So you can't simply check "greenness" in an index.) Greenness describes a quality of God's very being. In the beginning, Hildegard says, all of creation was green, and all the living things of nature contain God's greenness. She claimed that the beloved saints and her own vowed virgins are examples of life in this greenness. Even earthworms share in the greenness of the grass within which they live. When discussing jewel therapy(!), Hildegard claims that emeralds are the most useful gem, given that they are green. Her homilies intersperse scriptural citations with her own allegorical gloss, and several of these sermons deal with greenness in the gospels. In her Homily 19 on Matthew 8:1-13, Hildegard explicates the centurion's request that Jesus "say the word" as Jesus "kissing my flesh with your greenness," and in her Homily 26 on the prodigal son, the father is inspired to host the feast because "the greenness of the Holy Spirit has blossomed again in him."[5] Thus, all three persons of the Trinity—God as creator, savior, and vivifier—manifest and grant greenness.

It is always a danger—for example, in an essay such as this—when rereading the saints to make them say what we wish they had said; yet without making untoward claims for Hildegard's positions, we do encounter in her works a foundational appreciation for a green God and for God's life force in nature. There is here no romanticism, no evocation of charming flowers that bloom where we are not. Rather, even somewhat disgusting plants and repulsive animals contain God's greenness, and we honor God, nature, and humankind by careful attention to this *viriditas.*

There is now a considerable bibliography, including the words of Bartholomew I, the Ecumenical Patriarch of Constantinople, urging Christians to adopt ecological lifestyles. Adhering to the classic Western liturgy, worship planners can find various ways to highlight a green view of God's earth.[6] Some churches encourage the invention of entire worship services that focus on the appreciation of nature and a baptismal ecological ethic. So, what are my suggestions as to how *viriditas* might influence Sunday worship?

First of all, on the Sunday closest to Hildegard's death day of September 17, we can sing "O Holy Spirit, Root of Life,"[7] the hymn that Jean Janzen composed based on Hildegard's poems, especially #1, #2, and #24 in her *Symphony of the Harmony of Celestial Revelations*.[8]

We can reduce the reams of paper that we distribute at each liturgy and then throw away at noon on Sunday. We ought not pretend that this use of paper has nothing to do with greenness.

We can eliminate fake nature in our worship spaces, for example, by refusing any use of artificial flowers to adorn the sanctuary or artificial greens on windowsills in wintertime. Willing to face the issues that will arise, we will not at Christmastime set up artificial trees. We will replace those oil-burning plastic candle-things, which substitute ease of use for natural adornment, with either genuine candles or bowls of oil and wicks.

We can re-examine the parish practice of regularly purchasing flower arrangements from the local florist. I recall the church architect and designer Frank Kacmarcik referring to these matching bouquets as His and Hers displays. All too often these perfectly arranged flowers are out of season and bring into our assembly very little of God's creation. Might potted plants be greener?

The three-year ecumenical lectionary has helped restore the Sunday singing of the psalms, in many of which humans join with the rest of nature to praise God. Look, for example, at the three psalms appointed for Christmas. In Psalm 96, the earth, the sea, the fields, and all the trees are shouting for joy at the coming of God. Psalm 97 speaks of the earth, its islands, clouds and darkness, earthquakes and lightnings. In Psalm 98, the rivers are clapping their hands, and the hills are praising God. So not only angels and shepherds, but the whole of the green earth leads our incarnation song.

As one of the standard petitions in our assembly's intercessions, we can pray each week for the well-being of nature. And this is not merely to pray that humankind respect God's created order and be better stewards of God's gifts: we can also beg God to continue creation, to sustain a fragile earth, to give the polar bears ice on which to thrive, to reinvigorate the bee colonies, to heal the diseased Tasmanian devils of Australia. Perhaps an ecologically minded member of the community can assist the intercessor by suggesting an appropriate request for each week.

And because Hildegard was not concerned mainly with pretty nature, but with the ways God gives greenness in our daily lives, we can pray not only for fields of ripening grain, which perhaps some of the assembly have never even seen, but also for neighborhood grocery stores and for local farmers' markets.

"Heaven and earth are full of your glory," we sing each week. So at the table we can praise God for the greenness of this earth, so filled with divine glory. On Palm/Passion Sunday, we can distribute two-foot-long palm fronds to everyone, and during the Hosanna, we can all wave these fronds, as if to greet our Savior with the greenness of the earth that he rules.

At coffee hour, we can serve greener foods than are sometimes offered for our snacks, and on the Sunday closest to Hildegard's September 17, we can set out only green foods—grapes and celery sticks and snap peas and mints. We can do away with disposable cups and plates, since as green Christians, we need once again to learn how to wash dishes.

But most important in my mind is the bread and the wine.

In her primary theological work *Scivias*, Hildegard wrote about the elements of the Eucharist. As if recording God's words, she says that the bread is such that "they who receive it are bathed with heavenly light in soul and body and cleansed by faith from their inner uncleanness. It is fitting that His flesh should now be made from that fruit which is without the sap of bitterness. How? The grain of wheat is the strongest and best of all the fruits there are; it has in its stalk no sap or pith like other trees, but its stem rises to a spike that leads to the fruit, and it never produces bitter juice either in heat or in cold. . . . My Only-Begotten Son came forth in verdant integrity as the stalk brings forth the clustered grains of wheat."[9] Admittedly, this is not a twenty-first-century way to talk about bread, but it seems to me that her praise of the wheat in the eucharistic bread, her hope that we experience heavenly light, and her vision of "verdant integrity" would urge us to entomb forevermore the vague reminiscence of bread that is perhaps suggested by communion wafers and to return to the greenness of real bread, baked the day before the liturgy, broken and shared and consumed in thanksgiving for the food that God actually gives. (Yes, I feel strongly about this.) We celebrate the mystery best, it seems to me, not by assigning the presence of God to rarefied disks manufactured for altar use. Rather, we stand in awe of our embodied God, who feeds us divinity in, with, and under actual bread, perhaps round multigrain loaves, perhaps tortillas or oval Syrian flatbreads, perhaps pita from the convenience store, as the Spirit fills the church with Christ by means of the greenness of the life of this real earth.

Of eucharistic wine, Hildegard writes, "For as wine flows out of the vine, so My Son went forth from My heart. As that liquor comes out of the sweetest and strongest fruit of the vine, all merciful and true justice appears out of the Incarnation of My Son. Those who faithfully cleave to him are made by Him green and fruitful, so that they bring forth noble fruits of virtue."[10] Can we rejoice in this gift of the fruit of the vine, the communicants joining their hands with those of the minister of the cup to take hold of the stem of a numinous chalice, happily swallowing God's greenness?[11] Can we be done with the practice of intinction? The issues of welcoming recovering alcoholics and of convincing the assembly of sanitary usage remain contemporary pastoral concerns. Yet I urge those assemblies that serve only grape juice to everyone or that replace the common cup with individual glasses to strive to imbue these reduced current practices with the spirituality resonant in wine and the exceptionality of the one body of believers sharing in one cup.

Such lush descriptions of bread and wine Hildegard writes! I beg us: let us find ways to make the bread and the wine of our Communions proclamatory of God's greenness. Could we come away from Communion rejoicing at God's good creation? Perhaps at the Easter Vigil, the bread was baked in the preceding hours in the church's kitchen, and so accompanying our celebration of the first Eucharist of the Resurrection, we all can smell the greenness of the fresh bread. May it be such that communicants delight in our eating of bread and drinking of wine, while we find worthy ways to welcome at our tables those whose health requires that they refrain from partaking in the church's bread and wine.

"De te . . . terra viriditatem sudat."[12] From you, O fiery Spirit, writes the poet Hildegard, the earth exudes greenness. May our liturgies do the same.

Chapter 23

Recessing for Service
with Amy Carmichael

Eighteen-year-old Amy Carmichael, walking home from church with her widowed mother and siblings one Sunday morning in 1885, was distressed by the sight of a raggedly dressed elderly woman carrying a heavy bundle. Amy and her two brothers assisted the woman, and this memorable experience became the model for her life: first you worship, then you serve.

An Irish Presbyterian, Carmichael began her celebrated career as a lay Protestant missionary ministering among the poor "shawlies" in Belfast and Manchester—the mill women too poor to afford hats or, indeed, any clothes that were appropriate to wear to church. In 1896, after short stints in Japan and Ceylon, Carmichael settled in Dohnavur, a small town in southern India, where she dedicated fifty-five years as "Amma" to what became known as the Dohnavur Family. Carmichael had long been committed to participation in organized worship—Sunday services, Wednesday evening prayer meetings, home devotions, and private prayer. For Sunday worship at Dohnavur, held in both English and Tamil, she combined evangelical preaching, Methodist song, Quaker silence, and Anglican ritual. Eventually her compound included an orphanage, nurseries, a hospital, a school, dormitories, gardens, farm buildings, and a retreat center. She died on January 18, 1951, and is buried there on site. What is now termed the Dohnavur Fellowship is still serving those in dire need.[1]

Although during the nineteenth and twentieth centuries large numbers of missionaries served throughout the world—Protestant and Roman Catholic, lay, religious, and clergy—Amy Carmichael was one who became well known, thanks to her having published more than thirty-five books of heartfelt accounts of her ministry. She was the first author who included photographs of native life with her text. She scorned the popular Victorian romanticized view of missions as successfully Christianizing multitudes of quaint peoples. Her first book, *Things as They Are: Mission Work in Southern India*,[2] was upsetting to its readers, since she offered no glowing reports about plentiful conversions. Rather, in one affecting anecdote after another, she told of her extreme disappointments and frequent failures, describing her situation in India as perpetually hampered by the rigid caste system. To "break caste" was an Indian's greatest horror, and the community could either ostracize or indeed punish, to the death, someone who did: and to become a Christian was to break caste. Making no headway with high-caste Indians, Carmichael attended mostly to the "slaves of the gods," the young girls who, sometimes as infants, were dedicated to Hindu temples as servants, to become when of age religious prostitutes, as well as to those girls unwillingly sold into marriage bonds that sanctioned wife abuse. Thus, the earliest residents of her community were girls who had been rescued from such lives. Her writings urged Christians in the homeland to pray, pray, pray for the conversion of the Hindus. Yet throughout, she modeled a life marked by joy, and the communion services at the compound always concluded with the singing of "Jesus, Thou Joy of Loving Hearts."[3]

Reading about the lives of the saints, we often discover teachings with which we disagree, conduct we find unsettling, an understanding of the Christian life that is to us offensive. So with Carmichael: although she did wear a sari, she rejected any and all theology and religious ritual that in our time many Christians advocate as appropriate enculturation. "Identification with the people whom we have come to win is the aim of many a missionary, but the difficulty always is the same—climate and customs are dead against it: how can we do it?"[4] Rather, she maintained the most uncompromising attitudes of premodern conservative Protestantism. To her, there was no gray, only white or black. She denounced Hinduism, called its rituals idolatry, and judged the caste system totally evil. She disdained the methods of other Christian missionaries, and, condemning those Indians whom she labeled "nominal Christians," she authorized baptisms only after a catechumenal process of several years. Defending her policy, she wrote of Christ's command to baptize, "Did He not know the conditions of high-caste Hindu life in India when He gave this command? Was He ignorant of the breaking up of families which obedience to it would involve?"[5] For a convert to be rejected by family was, she maintained, only to be expected when following the Crucified. She claimed that Christ did not promise success. Rather, he called for obedience, and she expected of her Family total loyalty to her Master, which her people were to demonstrate by their absolute obedience to her. She believed that Jesus spoke to her daily, directing her decisions. In the 1940s, she judged that India was not ready for self-rule. Always she advocated the harder way as the only Christian way.

But I can laud one of Carmichael's favorite quotes, "Saved to serve."[6] Her life of service beckons to me over the miles and decades. So what about us, as we recess from Sunday worship?

Hoping for more thoughtful attention to the conclusion of our Eucharists, we now speak of the fourth part of the assembly's worship as the Sending. We do not merely leave. We are sent: from lying helplessly near the pool, we are now washed with the light of baptism to take up our mat and walk. Lutherans often refers to the liturgy as "the service." We recess from the service—that is, together we process out of worship—in order to continue our service to God outside the sanctuary. It is as if Monday through Saturday are only a recess—that is, a time-out—during which we serve our neighbor, only to return to our service on Sunday.

It has been a treasured Lutheran tradition to sing Simeon's *Nunc Dimittis* after each Communion. Simeon has held the child Jesus in his arms, and we have held the bread in our hands. Simeon has seen the infant Word, and we have received that Word. Simeon has beheld God's salvation, and looking around us in the assembled body, we too have seen how God saves. Simeon speaks of the light, and we remember our baptism. Simeon can go in peace toward death, and we too exit the service with God's blessing, prepared to meet death. The title of one biography of Carmichael, *A Chance to Die*, is taken from her warning to interested volunteers that "missionary work is simply a chance to die."[7] I have long taught that one purpose of Sunday worship is to ready ourselves for death. Following the cross, remembering the faithful departed, and accompanied by the call to discipleship, we go to serve this week and until we die.

As one of many Christians who write about liturgical spirituality, I am wary of what strike me as extravagant claims about the transformative power of worship, as if, were the liturgy to be absolute wow-land, the kingdom of God would magically appear on Sunday afternoon around the globe. Alas, it doesn't happen like that. As part of the Sending, I have always liked the dismissal adapted from 1 Thessalonians 5: "Go forth into the world to serve God with gladness; be of good courage; hold fast to that which is good; render to no one evil for evil; strengthen the fainthearted; support the weak; help the afflicted; honor all people; love and serve God, rejoicing in the power of the Holy Spirit." We rejoice in the power of the Holy Spirit, rather than the power of our parish liturgy—and Carmichael would agree with me about this.

Carmichael was far from alone in living between Sunday services in service to others. Here is a list of a few other Christians who have died since 1900, whose variety of service might inspire our recessing next Sunday.[8]

Clara Maass, a Lutheran nurse serving in urban and army hospitals, died in 1901 in Cuba as a result of having volunteered in a medical study of the transmission of yellow fever.

Elizabeth Wright, whose mother was of Cherokee descent and whose father was African American, established schools in the American South for African American children. An Episcopalian, she died in 1906.

Dying in 1912, Lottie Moon, an American Baptist, learned Mandarin and served as an educator and evangelist in Northern China, working especially with women and girls.

Harriet Tubman, "Moses of her people," was born into slavery and, after having escaped, made many trips back into slave country to lead dozens of other enslaved persons to freedom. Later, as a member of the African Methodist Episcopal Church, she joined with white women to advance rights for all women. She died in 1913.

"Blessed Assurance" is one of the eight thousand gospel hymns and sacred songs that the blind Methodist songster Fanny Crosby composed. She died in 1915.

Liliuokalani, the last queen of the Hawaiian Islands, died in 1917, having attempted to extend the franchise in her lands before being forced to abdicate in 1895. Over her lifetime, she was a member of several different Protestant churches.

A daughter of Nathaniel Hawthorne, Rose Hawthorne Lathrop, having become a Roman Catholic, was a nurse and founder of a religious congregation dedicated to the care of those incurably sick with cancer. She died in 1926.

Isabel Florence Hapgood, who died in 1928, a gifted linguist and translator of Orthodox liturgical texts, spent much of her energies encouraging ecumenical friendship between her Episcopal church and the Orthodox churches.

The Episcopalian Francis Gaudet died in 1934, having dedicated much energy to the reform of prisons in the American South.

One of many Christians who died in a Nazi concentration camp in 1945, the Russian Orthodox nun Maria Skobtsova had spent years caring for refugees in Paris and, during the German occupation, hiding Jews from capture.

Katherine Drexel founded a Roman Catholic religious order through which women served Native American and African

American children in schools supported by her family's immense wealth. She died in 1955.

Satoko Kitahara, called the Mary of Ants Town, joined her life with the ragpickers in the slums of Tokyo. "I experienced a desire amounting almost to a necessity to 'serve,' which seemed to be a natural accompaniment to being a follower of Christ." A Roman Catholic, she died of tuberculosis in 1958.

Lillian Thrasher, a member of the Assemblies of God who died in 1961, became known as "Mother of the Nile" in recognition of her care for sick and orphaned children in Egypt.

The Roman Catholic southern author Flannery O'Connor wrote fiction about the surprising reality of grace and died young in 1964. She once wrote, "What people don't realize is how much religion costs. They think faith is a big electric blanket, when of course it is the cross."[9]

Frances Perkins was the first woman to serve as a member of the cabinet of an American president. An Episcopalian, she was Secretary of Labor under President Franklin Delano Roosevelt, helping to establish the New Deal and the Social Security program, and died in 1965.

The Methodist minister Georgia Harkness, who died in 1974, was a theology professor, the author of thirty-seven books on the Christian life, and a promoter of ecumenism worldwide.

Pauli Murray, the first African American woman ordained a priest in the Episcopal Church, provided research that assisted Thurgood Marshall in the preparation of the *Brown v. Board of Education* Supreme Court decision in 1954. She died in 1985.

In 1997, Mother Teresa died, after decades of walking the streets of Calcutta each morning to bring back to her convent the sick and dying, so that the poorest of the poor could receive loving care in their last hours.

Ade Bethune, a Belgian baroness and a liturgical artist associated with the Catholic Worker Movement, served as artistic director of the Terra Sancta Guild and died in 2002.

And dying in 2005 was the African Methodist Episcopal Rosa Parks, who sat down in a bus in 1955 and for the next fifty years rose up to support the cause of civil rights.

(Perhaps too long a list: yet how many of your favorites did I miss?)

And there are the countless forgotten Christians, the regular folks who worshiped and then served—our great-aunts and grandmothers, our catechism instructors and Sunday school teachers, the multitudes who raised others' children and who cleaned others' toilets, the many thousands dead in childbirth, that little old lady who always sat in the back pew, the great cloud of witnesses who, while singing hymns and reciting prayers, did the work they were given to do, serving those who had been given them to serve.

Concerning her life of service, Carmichael said, "I would rather burn out than rust out,"[10] and in one of her poems wrote, "Make me thy fuel, Flame of God."[11] Shimmering words to remember, as we recess from service for service. But has our Sunday worship provided the sparks we need?

24
Chapter

Treasuring the Triduum with Egeria

geria is renowned for having undertaken extensive travels in Egypt, the Holy Land, and surrounding areas,
probably between 381 and 384, and for having composed an astonishingly significant journal describing many
aspects of her pilgrimage. She addressed her diary to "ladies,
reverend sisters":[1] so perhaps she was a member back home
in northwestern Spain of a community of pious women. That
she was what we call a nun is unlikely, granting the relatively
early date of her journey, her personal independence, and the
considerable financial means required for her three-year-long
adventure. Of her journal, only one manuscript copy from the
eleventh century has been found, and that in 1884. Although
missing several pages, the travelogue wins first prize as the
most valued description of Christian worship practices ever
penned by a woman.

Egeria described her visits to believers who were famous for
their sanctity or ecclesial position, and she reported on the liturgical practices in which she participated everywhere she
went. On her journey homeward, she took a three-day detour
to visit the shrine of Thecla, at her tomb participating in the
usual pattern of pilgrims: prayer, appropriate readings, more
prayer. But it is especially the details she provided of the worship in Jerusalem during Holy Week, as pilgrims honored
Christ in prayer and appropriate readings, that interest me here.

Egeria related the route between the stational liturgies that
took place during what she calls Great Week, recording details

of the liturgies and attendant rituals of Palm Sunday (chapters
30–31), Maundy Thursday (chapters 35–36), Good Friday
(chapter 37), and Easter itself (chapters 38–39). I smile especially at her report of the exposition on Good Friday of what
was honored as the True Cross, which pilgrims knelt to kiss;
the bishop and several deacons kept guard of the cross, since
the story was that previously a pious believer had taken a bite
out of it.[2] (Don't you wonder what happened to that pilgrim,
with such a mouthful of holiness?)

The clarity of Egeria's account makes evident her excitement
over the way Christians kept Holy Week in Jerusalem and her
desire to share her religious experiences with her community.
She comments repeatedly about her pleasure that the biblical
readings, psalms, hymns, and prayers were appropriately chosen to fit the location and the day, in this way the worshipers
able to recall Christ's life, passion, death, resurrection, and
ascension. Notwithstanding the richness of her descriptions
of the primary liturgies she attended, the intervening devotional services, and the processions from one stational site to
another, Egeria remains responsible for what must be the most
disappointing sentence in all of Christian historical texts, when
she recorded in summary fashion, "The Easter vigil is observed
here exactly as we observe it at home."[3] Period.

One of the most monumental changes brought about during
the twentieth century in the worship life of many churches has
been the restoration of the Triduum, those three days so treasured by Egeria and recently adapted for contemporary worshipers. But why am I here paying any attention to the Great
Three Days, if these essays mean to comment on the assembly's
worship on Sunday?

Because.

Because: a worthy parish celebration of the Triduum does
not remain within those three days, to be tucked away after
Easter in everyone's memory until next Holy Week. Rather,
the Great Three Days enhance the entire year. Christians have
come to recognize that every Sunday's worship is a celebration

of Christ's resurrection, and the Triduum offers its ritual treasury to enrich the worship of the faithful all year long. What follows here is a list of some of the ways that the Three Days can improve worship Sunday after Sunday.

The Triduum is about Christ: his life, passion, death, and resurrection. This centering in Christ reminds all worshipers that also at the weekly liturgy, the community gathers primarily to receive and renew its faith in Christ, rather than to observe lesser celebrations (Mother's Day?) or to focus on personal issues—despite an individualist culture that hopes that most things are mostly about the great Me.

The services of the Triduum require the collaboration of many participants, from those who ensure that the water for the footwashing is warm, to the group that sets up the cross for adoration, to the instrumentalists who accompany the Song of the Three Jews from the Prayer of Azariah, to the preacher who proclaims to the twenty-first century the meaning of Christ's salvation. This cadre of folks can continue their cooperation for regular worship throughout the year.

Although we are not pilgrims processing from one sacred site in Jerusalem to another, many parishes adapt the stational model described by Egeria by moving from one venue to another during the liturgies of these Three Days: the footwashing takes place in the narthex, the assembly follows the cross around the city block, the lighting of the fire is outside in the yard, the service of readings in the fellowship hall, the Eucharist in the sanctuary. Only the tiniest number of parishes have as a regular worshiper a member of the American Ballet Theatre who can dance at the Vigil as Miriam on the safe side of the sea, but perhaps your parish invites everyone to join a conga line as the choir sings Exodus 15:21. Can such movement of the people characteristic of the Triduum inspire us to get worshipers out of their seating on Sunday morning, so that worship is not mostly just sitting there? Can the assembly gather around the font for a baptism, process up the aisle with their offerings, encircle the altar for Communion?

Egeria's experience of the Great Week was unique to Jerusalem. Is anything especially characteristic, perhaps even unique, about how your assembly, in its location, with its participants, keeps the Three Days and then worships each Sunday?

Those Christians who use a lectionary are accustomed to having the readings appropriate to each day. And what about the remainder of the propers for each Sunday? Are all the hymns, the prayers, the intercessions, the vesture, the flower arrangements, the art in the space and on the handouts, appropriate to the day, as Egeria so appreciated?

Egeria explained that translations were provided for those Syriac-speaking worshipers who could not understand the Greek liturgies and that explanations were provided for those who spoke only Latin.[4] Our churches continue the often-controversial task of perpetual translation. But on each Sunday there is the further task of defining Christian language: what, for example, does the church mean by terms like salvation, heaven, grace? Is any such explanation provided somehow on Sunday mornings?

On Good Friday, we joined Mary and John at the foot of the cross to pray for everything and everyone in the world. Can the comprehensiveness of this bidding prayer encourage our weekly intercessions to attend to all those in need? The list is endless, and the choice of what to pray for this week a worthy ministry in itself.

Perhaps the youth group not only chose visuals to coordinate with the readings at the Vigil, but also operated the projection equipment. Their ministry can continue throughout the year. Can we use such technology to enhance each Sunday's worship with art or design?

That in the fourth century Easter was one of the primary occasions for baptism has led at least some churches to restore the baptismal emphasis of the Vigil. Scheduling a baptism at the Vigil gives the sacrament its due solemnity and surrounds it with appropriate celebration. What about the baptisms scheduled on other Sundays? How can a baptism that is held in the middle of August, because that's when the godparents can be present, exhibit some of the grandeur of the Easter rite?

The Triduum includes two quite distinctive celebrations of the Eucharist. On Maundy Thursday, we have before us the footwashing and the meal in the upper room, while at the Easter Vigil, we gather at the empty tomb after celebrating by the sea. The songs that accompany our meal will be appropriate to these two days. And perhaps the bread of Thursday is pita and its wine red, and the bread of the Vigil a freshly baked whole wheat loaf and the wine white. What about each Sunday of the year? Which bread, which wine? What is the tone of the Eucharist most appropriate to each Sunday?

Over the course of the Great Week, Egeria heard readings from all four of the gospels.[5] Those of us who use the ecumenical lectionary achieve this diversity over the course of three years. But do we remind worshipers which is the gospel that we are hearing each Sunday and what is its particular vision of Christ and of the believing community?

Many of the biblical readings Egeria heard were taken from the Old Testament. At the Vigil, some of these selections are the beloved narratives of the faith. But on many standard Sundays, the Old Testament selection is less accessible than is the stunning poem of creation or the dramatic escape from Egypt. Can we all year long clarify why these weekly passages were chosen and how they speak to our Christian life?

From Maundy Thursday through Easter, Egeria heard the whole of John 13:1–20:31. In our time, there is especially one characteristic of John's gospel that raises questions about its proclamation. Simply stated, John's use of the term "the Jews" needs pastoral attention. In various places in the readings of the Triduum, "the Jews" might refer to a crowd that urges the execution of Jesus (e.g., John 18:31), the temple authorities (e.g., 18:12), the adherents of a world religion (e.g., 19:21), or the residents of the province of Judea (e.g., 18:33).[6] Although our sermons ought not be largely footnotes to ancient Greek, ought our liturgical translation hint at these differences? Most scholars concur that the fourth gospel was composed by a Jewish Christian sometime around 100, by which time synagogues had begun to reject as members those who identified Jesus as the Messiah. Not surprisingly, the author and editors of the fourth gospel were intent on distinguishing Christian believers from those Jews who did not believe in Christ as the Logos of God. Whenever John is proclaimed—Christmas Day, the second Sunday after Epiphany, Lent in Year A, the Triduum, the Sundays of Easter, August in Year B—how can we inform our people about John's vocabulary and translate it for our time?

The notion of literal historicism, a tendency that is found in many of the world's religions, was intensified in Christianity by the practice of pilgrimages to the Holy Land. But I am grateful for the proclamation of John during the Three Days, because its preference for symbolic expression helps mute such fundamentalism. That the entire cohort of six hundred arresting soldiers fall down before the I AM of Jesus; that Jesus debates boldly with Pilate; that he is buried with a hundred pounds of spices in a garden: these are not literal descriptions of the passion and death of Jesus. Rather, John uses metaphors, sometimes outlandish, to proclaim that Jesus is the Logos, the Son of God, and such poetic language during the Triduum can prepare us for the extraordinary speech that is found in much of Scripture.

Surely Egeria's experience was enhanced by its taking place at the sacred sites of Jesus' life. By the fourth century, very few Jews lived in Jerusalem. The Emperor Constantine had spent vast sums of money, and his mother Queen Helena had directed archaeological digs of the city, to discover and celebrate its Christian history. Egeria was among the countless numbers of believers then and now who, to nurture their religious devotion or to expunge God's memory of their sins or to have the adventure of their lifetime, became pilgrims. Then and now they visit the genuine and the purported sites of the life of Jesus and his followers. It is likely that the Christianizing of the locations was significant in those early centuries as a mark of the end of persecution and martyrdom of the faithful.[7]

Still today there is an absolute industry in Christian pilgrimages to the Holy Land, some with a stated and perhaps controversial political intent. Some Christians carry the Holy Land back home, as if the vial of water from the Jordan River is holier than what rains down in our land. Yet surely in our time many tourists realize that they are viewing not the genuine locations of Christ's ministry, but rather—although this in itself might be a useful activity—the sites of centuries of Christian devotion.

But the Christian tradition as a whole rejected pilgrimage as a religious requirement, and theologians taught that each weekly local assembly of the faithful is the place where we encounter Christ. We need not kiss a relic thought to be the True Cross: according to the ecumenical usage on Good Friday, an assembly uses its own processional cross, or perhaps a cross crafted from local raw timbers, and it is this cross that the assembly symbolically reverences with these words: "Behold the life-giving cross, on which was hung the Savior of the whole world." Even in the fourth century, some theologians complained about the popularity of pilgrimage, as though God might be found more fully in some other place than the local assembly. Gregory of Nyssa was particularly peeved by the notion that the Holy Spirit "is plentifully present in Jerusalem, but unable to travel so far that he reaches us."[8] Indeed, without any travel in time or space, the Exultet sings, also in our twenty-first century, "This is the night."

So, what is the message concerning pilgrimage for every Sunday's worship? This liturgy is where Christ is found, God worshiped, the Spirit received. We do not need to hunt down hermits living in holy caves: the saints are around us on Sunday morning. As we strip the worship space on Good Friday, we can think of those who prepared Jesus' body for burial, and we transfer our devotion from Jerusalem to our own sanctuary. We stand to hear the gospel because Christ is speaking here in this room: ought it matter to anyone where some Christians imagine that Jesus was buried? All we need to touch is the hand of our neighbor at the peace; the only walk we need to take is up toward the altar for the bread and wine.

At one point in her journal, Egeria wrote, "You, my sisters, my light, kindly remember me, whether I live or die."[9] Egeria, we—your sisters and brothers—do remember you. We remember you remembering Thecla. We treasure your words; we treasure the Triduum. And we aim to instill our Sunday worship with the spirit of your pilgrimage.

Afterword

If you wish to thank God for these twenty-four voices, here is a calendar of dates appropriate for their commemoration:

January 18	Amy Carmichael, 1951
February 18	Martin Luther, 1546
March 7	Perpetua, c. 203
March 12	Symeon the New Theologian, 1022
March 21	Thomas Cranmer, 1556
April 23	Margaret Fell, 1702
April 29	Catherine of Siena, 1380
May 8	Julian of Norwich, c. 1416
June 1	Justin Martyr, c. 165
July 1	Catherine Winkworth, 1878
July 11	Benedict, 547
July 22	Mary Magdalene
August 10	Lawrence, 258
August 13	Radegund, 587
August 16	Brother Roger, 2005
September 17	Hildegard, 1179
September 30	Jerome, 420
October 4	Francis of Assisi, 1226
October 26	Philipp Nicolai, 1608
November 1	Egeria—on All Saints' Day
November 15	Johannes Kepler, 1630
November 29	Dorothy Day, 1980
December 4	John of Damascus, 749
December 7	Ambrose, 397

We all have our issues, and here is one of mine: Due to a twentieth-century decision about how to render the Latin term *per annum*, some Christians have adopted the word "ordinary" to refer to many of the year's Sundays. I refuse to use this term, since as a speaker of American English, I hear the word with its ordinary meaning: what is ordinary is something common, nothing special, "not particularly good," says the American Heritage Dictionary of the English Language. Ah, but for Christians, no Sunday is ordinary.

However, alas! the fact is that Christian liturgy in many places on any particular Sunday may indeed be not particularly good—the Trinity trivialized, the lectors untrained, the preaching paltry, the Communion perfunctory, the music lousy, the worshipers passive, the purpose of the event obscured. A visiting Christian may find the theology inadequate, the piety distasteful, the style alien, the deity too tiny to grasp. The ritual may seem far too meager to address in any adequate manner both the wretchedness of the human condition and the revelation of divine presence. Yet our God is one who deigned to resort to incarnation and who was lined up with criminals in death. The one who is Wholly Other, Reigning Wisdom, and Fiery Life has chosen to inhabit the very baptized folk who have gathered on this Sunday, our liturgical meagerness notwithstanding. As I now sing every Maundy Thursday, "We strain to glimpse your mercy seat and find you kneeling at our feet."[1] It is tempting to travel to extraordinary liturgical whoop-de-dos, but our religion reminds us that God is here this Sunday, in this assembly, with these Scriptures, in this bread and wine. So calm yourself, and get to church on Sunday, and next Sunday too.

Admittedly, this attitude is easier for me than for many of my readers, for I have never lived in any location where Sunday worship was impossibly bad. (And for some of you, it is. "God, save us," we sing each Sunday morning.) Indeed, for several periods of my life, the Sunday worship I attended has been mercifully fine, a weekly gift calling me back to faith. Yet then and now, I must trust to the staff at my local church, for I do not with any regularity make decisions about or take leadership roles during Sunday worship. When things get grim, and sometimes they do, I have relied on several practices to keep myself from screaming aloud: (1) memorize a psalm; (2) meditate on the seven deadly sins (pride, covetousness, lust, anger, gluttony, envy, sloth!); or (3) pray for everyone I have ever met—as did Bishop Polycarp in 156, who, praying for "all those who had ever come into contact with him, both important and insignificant, famous and obscure, and the entire Catholic Church scattered through the world,"[2] made the arresting officers wait for over two hours, until with his prayers finally completed, they led him off to martyrdom. As I told a Hindu friend about Christian worship, it's the same every Sunday; it's different every Sunday. The immeasurable diversity in Christian Sunday mornings is a weekly reminder that God is bigger than this assembly, this church body, this ethnicity, this culture, this century. And in these essays, you have seen that sometimes I delight to listen to the bones of the faithful departed, rattling some life back into us all.

In one of my favorite sermons of all time, Augustine preached about the three stories of Jesus raising the dead.[3] Jesus brought back to life the daughter of the ruler of the synagogue, who had only just died; he returned life to the widow's son, who was being carried to the grave; and he raised Lazarus, who had been dead for four days. And Augustine said, Which one are you? Are you newly dead, or in your coffin on the way to the grave, or already stinking? To those who plan Sunday worship, indeed, to all the baptized, Augustine calls over the centuries: who or what is sleeping so deeply as to be dead dead dead? Sleeper, awake! Rise from the dead, and Christ will shine on you.

Thanks for that sermon, Augustine. We promise to remember it next Sunday.

Augustine's Day, August 28, 2017

Acknowledgments

There is no way that these essays could have achieved whatever scholarly respectability they have without my regular visits to the exemplary Bishop Payne Library at the Virginia Theological Seminary, Alexandria, Virginia. For the hospitality extended to me and the assistance of especially its director Mitzi Budde, I am exceedingly grateful.

Thanks to Bernadette Gasslein, editor of the journal *Worship*, for publishing six of these essays as the column "Amen Corner." My gratitude goes to Hans Christoffersen, publisher at Liturgical Press, for endorsing my proposal to extend the pattern of the six "Amen Corner" essays into a collection of twenty-four essays entitled *Saints on Sunday*. He is as gracious as the Benedictines he serves. I am indebted to the staff of Liturgical Press, especially Stephanie Lancour, for preparation of this publication.

My preparatory work for *More Days for Praise* (Augsburg Fortress, 2016), a guide to the calendar of commemorations of the Evangelical Lutheran Church in America, filled my ears with the voices of the saints and prepared my mind for this project. Both the Liturgical Language seminar and the Washington, DC, cohort of the North American Academy of Liturgy supported me in this project and assisted with several of the essays. Thomas McGonigle, OP, taught me to connect the spirituality of the saints with the intentions of the liturgy. Miriam Schmidt and Rosemary Sixbey cheered me on and offered insightful suggestions. Each essay benefited from careful and critical reading by Gordon Lathrop, saving my pages from various errors and infelicities. To these, among others, I am beholden.

Notes

Preface

1. Obituary of Marcus Borg, *Washington Post*, January 22, 2015.

Chapter 1—pages 1–7

1. Eric Francis Osborn, *Justin Martyr* (Tübingen, Germany: Mohr, 1973), 171.

2. This translation of Justin's First Apology is from Gordon W. Lathrop, *Holy Things: A Liturgical Theology* (Minneapolis: Fortress Press, 1993), 45.

3. See Colin Buchanan, "Questions Liturgists Would Like to Ask Justin Martyr," in *Justin Martyr and His Worlds*, ed. Sara Parvis and Paul Foster (Minneapolis: Fortress Press, 2007), 152–59.

4. Willy Rordorf, *Sunday: The History of the Day of Rest and Worship in the Earliest Centuries of the Christian Church* (Philadelphia: Westminster Press, 1968), 154–62.

5. Ibid., 109.

6. Abraham Joshua Heschel, *The Sabbath: Its Meaning for Modern Man* (New York: Farrar, Straus and Giroux, 1951), 22–23.

7. Wayne Muller, *Sabbath: Restoring the Sacred Rhythm of Rest* (New York: Bantam Books, 1999), 8.

8. Rordorf, *Sunday,* 290–91.

9. See the eucharistic prayer of Luther D. Reed, *The Lutheran Liturgy* (Philadelphia: Fortress Press, 1947), 356–57.

10. Justin, "Dialogue with Trypho, a Jew," chaps. 110 and 117, *The Ante-Nicene Fathers* (Grand Rapids, MI: Eerdmans, 1969), I: 254a and 258a.

Chapter 2—pages 8–13

1. Don Brophy, *Catherine of Siena: A Passionate Life* (New York: Blue Bridge, 2010).

2. Catherine of Siena, *The Dialogue*, trans. Suzanne Noffke (New York: Paulist Press, 1980), 364–66.

3. Suzanne Noffke, ed., *The Prayers of Catherine of Siena* (New York: Paulist Press, 1983), 54.

4. Ibid., 99–105.

5. "Triple Praise" is available in several publications, including Gail Ramshaw, *Pray, Praise, and Give Thanks: A Collection of Litanies, Laments, and Thanksgivings at Font and Table* (Minneapolis: Augsburg Fortress, 2017), 54–56.

6. Noffke, *The Prayers*, 42.

7. Catherine of Siena, *The Dialogue*, 49; Noffke, *The Prayers*, 16, 42.

8. Noffke, *The Prayers*, 42.

9. Hildegard of Bingen, "Vision Two, The Trinity," *Scivias,* 2:2, trans. Mother Columba Hart and Jane Bishop (New York: Paulist Press, 1990), 161.

10. Hildegard of Bingen, "Vision Six, Christ's Sacrifice and the Church," 6:44, 263.

11. Elisabeth of Schönau, "Visions—Book Two," *Medieval Women's Visionary Literature,* trans. Thalia A. Pandiri, ed. Elizabeth Alvilda Petroff (New York: Oxford University Press, 1986), 160.

12. Gertrude of Helfta, *The Herald of Divine Love*, III:18, trans. Margaret Winkworth (New York: Paulist Press, 1993), 176–77.

13. Marguerite Porete, *The Mirror of Simple Souls*, ch. 115, trans. Ellen L. Babinsky (New York: Paulist Press, 1993), 185.

14. Mechthild of Magdeburg, *The Flowing Light of the Godhead*, III:9, trans. Frank Tobin (New York: Paulist Press, 1998), 114.

15. Nicholas Watson and Jacqueline Jenkins, eds., "A Revelation of Love," *The Writings of Julian of Norwich*, ch. 54 (University Park, PA: Pennsylvania State University Press, 2006), 297.

16. Ibid., chap. 58, 307.

17. See, for example, Hannah Bacon, Karen Baker-Fletcher, Ruth Duck, Anne Hunt, Elizabeth A. Johnson, Catherine LaCugna, and Sallie McFague.

18. Joseph Jungmann, *The Mass of the Roman Rite* (New York: Benziger Brothers, 1959), 248–49. For further exposition, see Geoffrey Wainwright, " 'Son of God' in Liturgical Doxologies," in *Jesus, Son of God?*, *Concilium* 153, 3/1982, eds. Edward Schillebeeckx and Johannes-Baptist Metz (New York: Seabury Press, 1982), 49–54.

19. Ellen Wales Walpole, *The Golden Dictionary* (New York: Simon and Schuster, 1944), 31, 37, 53.

20. I credit the Methodist liturgical scholar James White for this anecdote.

21. "My Soul Proclaims Your Greatness," *Evangelical Lutheran Worship* (Minneapolis: Augsburg Fortress, 2006), #251, st. 3.

22. Peter Galadza, ed., *The Divine Liturgy: An Anthology for Worship* (Ottawa: Metropolitan Andrey Sheptytsky Institute of Eastern Christian Studies, 2004), 75 and passim.

23. "Prayer 3," from *The Book of Common Prayer 2004*, in *Anglican Eucharistic Liturgies 1985–2010*, ed. Colin Buchanan (Norwich, UK: Canterbury Press, 2011), 83.

24. "Holy Baptism," *Evangelical Lutheran Worship*, 230, emended.

25. Augustine, *The Trinity*, 10:14, trans. Mary T. Clark (New York: Paulist Press, 1984), 330.

26. "Come, Thou Almighty King," *Evangelical Lutheran Worship*, #408.

27. "Mothering God, You Gave Me Birth," *Evangelical Lutheran Worship*, #735.

28. "Source and Sovereign, Rock and Cloud," *Glory to God* (Louisville: Westminster John Knox Press, 2013), #11.

29. See, for example, www.skete.com.

30. Hildegard of Bingen's image, www.en.wikipedia.org, "Scivias."

31. Catherine of Siena, *The Dialogue*, 366.

Chapter 3—pages 14–19

1. John K. Ryan, trans., *The Confessions of St. Augustine* (New York: Doubleday, 1960), 130–31.

2. See Leonhard Goppelt, *Typos: The Typological Interpretation of the Old Testament in the New*, trans. Donald H. Madvig (Grand Rapids, MI: Eerdmans, 1982).

3. Michael Cameron, *Christ Meets Me Everywhere: Augustine's Early Figurative Exegesis* (Oxford: Oxford University Press, 2012), 11, 17–18, 24–29.

4. Genesis 22, Exodus 14–15, Jonah 1, and Daniel 3 are among the twelve Vigil readings suggested in *Evangelical Lutheran Worship*, 269.

5. See Paul Ricoeur, *The Rule of Metaphor: Multi-displinary Studies of the Creation of Meaning in Language*, trans. Robert Czerny (Toronto: University of Toronto Press, 1975).

6. Roy J. Deferrari, trans., "The Sacraments," 1:13-15, in *Saint Ambrose, Theological and Dogmatic Works*, *The Fathers of the Church: A New Translation*, vol. 44 (Washington DC: Catholic University of America, 1963), 274.

7. "The Mysteries," 3:14, ibid., 10.

8. "The Holy Spirit," 14:147, ibid., 88.

9. Saint Ambrose of Milan, *Exposition of the Holy Gospel According to Saint Luke*, 7:180, trans. Theodosia Tomkinson (Etna, CA: Center for Traditionalist Orthodox Studies, 2003), 309.

10. Jerome as cited in Boniface Ramsey, *Ambrose* (New York: Routledge, 1997), 53.

11. See, for example, *The Bible of the Poor, Facsimile*, eds. Albert C. Labriola and John W. Smeltz (Pittsburgh: Duquesne University Press, 1990), 41, 43.

12. Philip Wheelwright, *Metaphor and Reality* (Bloomington: Indiana University Press, 1962), 47, cites liturgy as an example of tensive language.

13. Craig Alan Satterlee, *Ambrose of Milan's Method of Mystagogical Preaching* (Collegeville, MN: Liturgical Press, 2002), 221–22.

14. Harry Emerson Fosdick, "What Is the Matter with Preaching?" *Harper's Magazine*, reprinted in *Harry Emerson's Fosdick's Art of Preaching: An Anthology*, ed. Lionel Crocker (Springfield, IL: Charles C. Thomas, 1971), 30.

15. One contemporary translation is "O Splendor of God's Glory Bright," *Evangelical Lutheran Worship*, #559.

16. "Savior of the Nations, Come," *Evangelical Lutheran Worship*, #263.

17. Sylvia Dunstan, "You, Lord, Are Both Lamb and Shepherd," *Glory to God*, #274.

18. "Alleluia! Jesus Is Risen," *Evangelical Lutheran Worship*, #377.

19. M. F. Toal, trans. and ed., *The Sunday Sermons of the Great Fathers* (Chicago: Henry Regnery, 1963), IV:64-65.

20. Toal, trans. and ed., *The Sunday Sermons of the Great Fathers* (Chicago: Henry Regnery, 1957), I:213.

Chapter 4—pages 20–26

1. H. J. M. Turner, ed. and trans., *The Epistles of St. Symeon the New Theologian* (New York: Oxford University Press, 2009), 173–75.

2. Hymn 44, St. Symeon the New Theologian, *Hymns of Divine Love*, trans. George A. Maloney (Denville, NJ: Dimension Books, 1976), 227.

3. "Mystical Prayer of Our Father Saint Symeon," ibid., 9.

4. Hymn 47, ibid., 239.

5. Hymn 30, ibid., 170.

6. Owen Collins, ed., *2000 Years of Classic Christian Prayers: A Collection for Public and Personal Use* (Maryknoll, NY: Orbis Books, 1999), 41.

7. Elizabeth A. Johnson, *She Who Is: The Mystery of God in Feminist Theological Discourse* (New York: Crossroad, 1992), 148.

8. Gail Ramshaw, "Pronouns and the Christian God," *God beyond Gender: Feminist Christian God-Language* (Minneapolis: Fortress Press, 1995), 23–32.

9. "Sweet Delight, Most Lovely," *The New Century Hymnal* (Cleveland, OH: Pilgrim Press, 1995), #269.

10. "Spirit of Gentleness," *Evangelical Lutheran Worship*, #396.

11. "Loving Spirit," *Evangelical Lutheran Worship*, #397.

12. "God of Tempest, God of Whirlwind," *Evangelical Lutheran Worship*, #400.

13. "Like the Murmur of the Dove's Song," *Evangelical Lutheran Worship*, #403.

14. Symeon the New Theologian, *The Discourses,* trans. C. J. de Catanzaro (New York: Paulist Press, 1980), 341.

Chapter 5—pages 27–33

1. The most comprehensive study is Thomas J. Heffernan, *The Passion of Perpetua and Felicity* (New York: Oxford University Press, 2012). His translation of the passion is pps. 125–38.

2. Ross S. Kraemer and Shira L. Lander, "Perpetua and Felicitas," *The Early Christian World*, ed. Philip F. Esler (New York: Routledge, 2000), II: 1048–68.

3. See Heffernan, *Passion of Perpetua*, 176, for why he prefers "serpent."

4. For example, see the life-sized temptation of Adam and Eve crafted by the workshop of Luca della Robbia in the Walters Art Gallery, Baltimore, MD.

5. See Gustaf Aulén, *Christus Victor*, trans. A. G. Hebert (New York: Macmillan, 1934), 38–44.

6. Philip C. Almond, *The Devil: A New Biography* (Ithaca, NY: Cornell University Press, 2014), 196–206.

7. See, for example, Richard Beck, *Reviving Old Scratch: Demons and the Devil for Doubters and the Disenchanted* (Minneapolis: Fortress Press, 2016), 29–36.

8. Paul W. Harkins, trans. and ed., *St. John Chrysostom: Baptismal Instructions*, Ancient Christian Writers No. 31 (New York: Newman Press, 1963), 48, 168.

9. Ibid., 93.

10. *Evangelical Lutheran Worship*, 229.

11. *The Book of Alternative Services of the Anglican Church of Canada* (Toronto: Anglican Book Centre, 1985), 154.

12. Max Thurian and Geoffrey Wainwright, eds., "The Liturgies of Baptism, The Eastern Orthodox Tradition," *Baptism and Eucharist: Ecumenical Convergence in Celebration* (Grand Rapids, MI: Eerdmans, 1983), 10.

13. *Glory to God* (Louisville: Westminster John Knox Press, 2013), 16.

14. *The Rites of the Catholic Church* (New York: Pueblo Publishing Company, 1976), 98–99.

15. Mark Searle, ed., *Alternative Futures for Worship*, vol. 2, *Baptism and Confirmation*, ed. (Collegeville, MN: Liturgical Press, 1987), 151.

16. Jane Howard, *Margaret Mead: A Life* (New York: Simon and Schuster, 1984), 348.

17. "A Mighty Fortress Is Our God," *Evangelical Lutheran Worship*, #505.

18. "Christ Jesus Lay in Death's Strong Bands," *Evangelical Lutheran Worship*, #370.

19. "Creator Spirit, Heavenly Dove," *Evangelical Lutheran Worship*, #577.

20. "God Rest You Merry, Gentlemen," *One in Faith* (Franklin Park, IL: World Library Publications, 2014), #391.

21. "When Peace Like a River," *Evangelical Lutheran Worship*, #785.

22. Robert Muchembled, *Damned: An Illustrated History of the Devil* (San Francisco: Seuil Chronicle, 2004), 167–68.

23. I have tried to accomplish this in "A Litany of Sorrows and Sins," *Pray, Praise, and Give Thanks*, 16–18.

Chapter 6—pages 34–40

1. See *The Annotated Luther*, vol. 1, *The Roots of Reform*, ed. Timothy J. Wengert (Minneapolis: Fortress Press, 2015), for new translations of the primary writings of Luther from his Ninety-Five Theses to "The Freedom of a Christian."

2. "Christian Questions with Their Answers," *A Short Explanation of Dr. Martin Luther's Small Catechism: A Handbook of Christian Doctrine* (St. Louis: Concordia Publishing House, 1943), 31–35.

3. "Confession and Forgiveness," *Evangelical Lutheran Worship*, 95.

4. A thoughtful feminist discussion of sin is Deanne A. Thompson, *Crossing the Divide: Luther, Feminism, and the Cross* (Minneapolis: Fortress Press, 2004), 108–10.

5. Nadia Bolz-Weber, *Pastrix: The Cranky, Beautiful Faith of a Sinner & Saint* (New York: Jericho Books, 2013), 74.

6. Kimberly Bracken Long, ed., *Feasting on the Word Worship Companion* (Louisville: Westminster John Knox Press, 2015).

7. For example, *Sundays and Seasons, Year C 2016* (Minneapolis: Augsburg Fortress, 2015), 206.

8. Laurence Hull Stookey, "Corporate Prayers of Confession," *Let the Whole Church Say Amen! A Guide for Those Who Pray in Public* (Nashville: Abingdon, 2001), 60.

9. Rabbi Jules Harlow, ed., Evening Service for Yom Kippur, *Maḥzor for Rosh Hashanah and Yom Kippur: A Prayer Book for the Days of Awe* (New York: The Rabbinical Assembly, 1972), 377–79.

10. Rabbi Delphine Horvilleur, "The Jewish 'ABC Song,'" *We Have Sinned: Sin and Confession in Judaism, Ashamnu and Al Chet*, ed. Rabbi Lawrence A. Hoffman (Woodstock, VT: Jewish Lights Publishing, 2012), 176–80.

11. Martin Buber, "The Alphabet," *Tales of the Hasidim: The Later Masters* (New York: Schocken Books, 1948), 292.

12. "Lord Jesus, Think on Me," *Evangelical Lutheran Worship*, #599.

13. "Out of the Depths," *Evangelical Lutheran Worship*, #600.

14. "Your Heart, O God, Is Grieved," *Evangelical Lutheran Worship*, #602.

15. "Amazing Grace," *Evangelical Lutheran Worship*, #779.

16. Frederick W. Faber, "There's a Wideness in God's Mercy," *Evangelical Lutheran Worship*, #587.

17. Kevin Nichols, "Our Father, We Have Wandered," *Evangelical Lutheran Worship*, #606.

18. Rosamond E. Herklots, "Forgive Our Sins, as We Forgive," *Evangelical Lutheran Worship*, #605.

19. "Son of God, Whose Heart Is Peace," *Glory to God*, #425.

Chapter 7—pages 41–48

1. Sally Bruyneel, *Margaret Fell and the End of Time: The Theology of the Mother of Quakerism* (Waco, TX: Baylor University Press, 2010), especially 77–117.

2. Ibid., 17, 81–83.

3. *Womens Speaking Justified* is available at www.qhpress.org/texts/fell.html.

4. *Guide to Being a Trans Ally*, online resource, PFLAG National, 2014.

5. Margaret Fell, "An Epistle of M. Fell to Friends, 1654," *Hidden in Plain Sight: Quaker Women's Writings 1650-1700*, ed. Mary Garman, Judith Applegate, Margaret Benefiel, and Dortha Meredith (Wallingford, PA: Pendle Hill Publications, 1996), 457.

Chapter 8—pages 49–55

1. See Amy Frykholm, *Julian of Norwich: A Contemplative Biography* (Brewster, MA: Paraclete Press, 2010), 100.

2. For the authoritative Middle English text with notes, see Nicholas Watson and Jacqueline Jenkins, eds., *The Writings of Julian of Norwich: A Vision Showed to a Devout Woman and a Revelation of Love* (University Park, PA: Pennsylvania State University Press, 2006). For ease of reading but with close rendering of the original, see James Walsh, trans., *The Revelations of Divine Love of Julian of Norwich* (Trabuco Canyon, CA: Source Books, 1961).

3. See Caroline Walker Bynum, *Jesus as Mother: Studies in the Spirituality of the High Middle Ages* (Berkeley: University of California Press, 1982), 112–13.

4. Watson and Jenkins, *Writings of Julian of Norwich*, 3.

5. Walsh, *Revelations of Divine Love*, chaps. 58–59, 158–62.

6. See Kerrie Hide, *Gifted Origins to Graced Fulfillment: The Soteriology of Julian of Norwich* (Collegeville, MN: Liturgical Press, 2001), 132–36.

7. Walsh, *Revelations of Divine Love*, chap. 17, 76.

8. Ibid., chap. 22, 83.

9. For the authoritative Middle English text with notes, see Barry Windeatt, ed., *The Book of Margery Kempe*, annotated edition (Rochester, NY: D.S. Brewer, 2000). For ease of reading but with close rendering of the original, see an edition translated by B. A. Windeatt, *The Book of Margery Kempe* (New York: Penguin Books, 1985).

10. Windeatt, *Book of Margery Kempe*, chap. 35, (1985), 122–25.

11. Ibid., chap. 36, 127.

12. Ibid., chap. 31, 114.

13. I warn against those editions that recast "this creature" as "I."

14. Windeatt, *Book of Margery Kempe*, chap. 78, 225.

15. Ibid., chap. 52, 163.

16. Ibid., chap. 65, 200.

17. Ibid., chap. 18, 78.

18. Sally Fitzgerald, ed., *The Habit of Being: The Letters of Flannery O'Connor* (New York: Vintage Books, 1979), 422.

19. Randall Balmer, *Mine Eyes Have Seen the Glory* (Worcester, PA: Gateway Films/Visions Video, 1992).

20. Susan Cain, *Quiet: The Power of Introverts in a World That Can't Stop Talking* (New York: Broadway Random House, 2012).

21. Watson and Jenkins, *Writings of Julian of Norwich*, ch. 86:2–5, 208.

22. Windeatt, *Book of Margery Kempe,* ch. 89, 261.

Chapter 9—pages 56–62

1. Catherine Winkworth, trans., *Lyra Germanica: Hymns for the Sundays and Chief Festivals of the Christian Year* (New York: Thomas N. Stanford, 1856), 57.

2. Ibid., 70.

3. Ibid., 106.

4. Ibid., 220.

5. Ibid., 241.

6. "Jesus, Priceless Treasure," *Evangelical Lutheran Worship*, #775.

7. Roland H. Worth Jr., *Bible Translations: A History through Source Documents* (Jefferson, NC: McFarland and Company, 1992), 29.

8. Ibid., 45.

9. Ibid., 115.

10. See Peter Jeffery, *Translating Tradition: A Chant Historian Reads "Liturgiam Authenticam,"* (Collegeville, MN: Liturgical Press, 2005) as an example of the debate.

11. Edited and published in *Worship* 52 (1978): 517–42.

12. See John B. Cobb, *Jesus' Abba: The God Who Has Not Failed* (Minneapolis: Fortress Press, 2015).

13. For example, Catherine Winkworth, trans., *Lyra Germanica: Second Series, The Christian Life*, (London: Longman, Green, Longman, Roberts, and Green, 1863), 63, 87.

14. Ibid., 62.

15. Cesáreo Gabaráin, "You Have Come Down to the Lakeshore," trans. Madeleine Forell Marshall, *Evangelical Lutheran Worship*, #817.

16. Harriet Lutsky, "Shadday as a Goddess Epithet," *Vetus Testamentum* 48 (1998): 15–36.

17. Winkworth, *Lyra Germanica*, 5.

18. Ibid., 17.

19. Ibid., 85.

20. Winkworth, *Lyra Germanica: Second Series*, 155.

21. Catherine Winkworth, *Christian Singers of Germany*, 1966, Essay Index Reprint Series (Freeport, NY: Books for Libraries Press, 1972), 288.

22. Winkworth, *Lyra Germanica: Second Series*, 177.

23. For both the Lakota and the English, see "Wakantanka Taku Nitawa," *The New Century Hymnal*, #3.

24. William K. Powers, *Oglala Religion* (Lincoln: University of Nebraska Press, 1975), 16, 45.

25. Ibid., 202.

26. See the two versions of "Praise to the Lord, the Almighty," *Evangelical Lutheran Worship*, #858 and #859.

27. Winkworth, *Christian Singers of Germany*, 89.

Chapter 10—pages 63–69

1. Raymond E. Brown, Joseph A. Fitzmyer, and Roland E. Murphy, ed., *The Jerome Biblical Commentary*, (Englewood Cliffs, NJ: Prentice-Hall, 1968), and *The New Jerome Biblical Commentary* (Englewood Cliffs, NJ: Prentice-Hall, 1989).

2. J. N. D. Kelly, *Jerome: His Life, Writings, and Controversies* (London: Duckworth, 1975), 337–39, argues for the earlier date of 331.

3. Jerome, Letter 18 A, in *The Christian Reader*, eds. Mary Gerhart and Fabian E. Idoh (Chicago: University of Chicago Press, 2007), 42.

4. Jerome, "The Meaning of the Gospel," *The Sunday Sermons of the Great Doctors*, trans. and ed. M. F. Toal (Chicago: Henry Regnery, 1958), II: 173.

5. Stefan Rebenich, *Jerome* (New York: Routledge 2002), 56–57.

6. Jerome, *Sunday Sermons*, II: 174.

7. Jerome *Christian Reader*, 40.

8. Paul M. van Buren, *According to the Scriptures: The Origins of the Gospel and of the Church's Old Testament* (Grand Rapids, MI: Eerdmans, 1998), 8, 87–88.

9. See Gail Ramshaw, "The First Testament in Christian Lectionaries," *Worship* 64 (1990), 494–510—which article failed to convince the church to replace "Old Testament" with "First Testament."

10. Jerome, "As the Hind Longs for the Running Water," *The Paschal Mystery: Ancient Liturgies and Patristic Texts,* ed. A. Hamman (Staten Island, NY: Alba House, 1969), 140–41.

Chapter 11—pages 70–75

1. T. F. Lindsay, *Saint Benedict: His Life and Work* (London: Burns Oates, 1949), 149.

2. Marion J. Hatchett, *Commentary on the American Prayer Book* (Minneapolis: Seabury Press, 1980), 327.

3. Thanks for these fine words to Irene Nowell, *Sing a New Song: The Psalms in the Sunday Lectionary* (Collegeville, MN: Liturgical Press, 1993), 2.

4. Harry P. Nasuti, "The Sacramental Function of the Psalms in Contemporary Scholarship and Liturgical Practice," in *Psalms and Practice:*

Worship, Virtue, and Authority, ed. Stephen Breck Reid (Collegeville, MN: Liturgical Press, 2001), 81.

5. Robert D. Putnam, *Bowling Alone: The Collapse and Revival of American Community* (New York: Simon and Schuster, 2001).

6. Abbot Justin McCann, *Saint Benedict*, rev. ed. (Garden City, NY: Image Doubleday, 1958), 74.

7. Jean Danielou, *The Bible and the Liturgy* (Notre Dame: University of Notre Dame Press, 1956), 177–90.

8. Leonard Doyle, trans., *The Rule of Saint Benedict 1980* (Collegeville, MN: Liturgical Press, 2001), 71.

Chapter 12—pages 76–82

1. Susan Haskins, *Mary Magdalen: Myth and Metaphor* (Old Saybrook, CT: Konecky and Konecky, 1993), 192–365.

2. Gail Ramshaw, *Christ in Sacred Speech: The Meaning of Liturgical Language* (Philadelphia: Fortress Press, 1986), 98–102, and *Reviving Sacred Speech: The Meaning of Liturgical Language* (Akron, OH: OSL Publications, 2000), 142–45.

3. Haskins, *Mary Magdalen* 98–191.

4. Google, "Eric Gill Nuptials of God."

5. David Mycoff, trans. and annotator, *The Life of Saint Mary Magdalene and of Her Sister Saint Martha* (Kalamazoo, MI: Cistercian Publications, 1989), from *PL* 112:1431–1508.

6. Ibid., 98.

7. See my efforts in this regard in *More Days for Praise: Festivals and Commemorations in Evangelical Lutheran Worship* (Minneapolis: Augsburg Fortress, 2016).

8. Mycoff, *Life of Saint Mary Magdalene*, 66.

9. Ibid., 72.

10. Ibid., 79.

11. Ibid., 85.

12. "By All Your Saints," *Evangelical Lutheran Worship*, #421, st. 16.

13. Austin B. Tucker, *The Preacher as Storyteller: The Power of Narrative in the Pulpit* (Nashville: B&H Publishing Group, 2008), 45.

14. See, for example, Joel B. Green and Michael Pasquarello III, eds., *Narrative Reading, Narrative Preaching: Reuniting New Testament Interpretation and Proclamation* (Grand Rapids, MI: Baker Academic, 2003) or Austin B. Tucker, *The Preacher as Storyteller: The Power of Narrative in the Pulpit* (Nashville: B&H Publishing, 2008).

15. Lisa Wilson Davison, "The First Apostle," *Preaching the Women of the Bible* (St. Louis: Chalice Press, 2006), 109–115.

16. Bruce Chilton, *Mary Magdalene: A Biography* (New York: Doubleday, 2005), 4.

17. Haskins, *Mary Magdalen*, 399, cites one such sermon, preached by Rev. John Damm, who was my pastor for many years.

18. Mycoff, *Life of Saint Mary Magdalene*, 81.

Chapter 13—pages 83–89

1. Marie Anne Mayeski, *Women at the Table: Three Medieval Theologians* (Collegeville, MN: Liturgical Press, 2004), 105–47.

2. "Sing, My Tongue," *Evangelical Lutheran Worship*, #355.

3. "The Royal Banners Forward Go," *The Hymnal 1982* (New York: The Church Hymnal Corporation, 1985), #162.

4. "O Cross of Christ, Immortal Tree," *One in Faith*, #676.

5. Király Imre von Pécselyi, "There in God's Garden," trans. Erik Routley, *Evangelical Lutheran Worship*, #342.

6. See Gustaf Aulén, *Christus Victor: An Historical Study of the Three Main Types of the Idea of the Atonement*, trans. A. G. Hebert (New York: Macmillan, 1969).

7. C. S. Lewis, *The Lion, the Witch, and the Wardrobe* (New York: Macmillan, 1950), 132–33.

8. Ibid., 113–15.

9. Mechthild of Magdeburg, *The Flowing Light of the Godhead*, III:9, trans. Frank Tobin (New York: Paulist Press, 1998), 59.

10. "The Pasch History," *The Paschal Mystery: Ancient Liturgies and Patristic Texts*, 64–65.

11. See Robin M. Jensen, *The Cross: History, Art, and Controversy* (Cambridge, MA: Harvard University Press, 2017), 123–49, and Christopher Irvine, *The Cross and Creation in Christian Liturgy and Art* (Collegeville, MN: Liturgical Press, 2013), 170–204, for Christian examples of the archetypal tree of life.

12. G. Ronald Murphy, *Tree of Salvation: Yggdrasil and the Cross in the North* (New York: Oxford University Press, 2013).

13. Brian Wildsmith, *The True Cross* (New York: Oxford University Press, 1977). Nine images depict this legend in John Plummer, *The Hours of Catherine of Cleves*, facsimile edition (New York: George Braziller, 1966), #79–87.

14. See Gail Ramshaw, *Treasures Old and New: Images in the Lectionary* (Minneapolis: Fortress Press, 2002), 393–400.

15. "Sing, My Tongue," *Evangelical Lutheran Worship*, # 355.

Chapter 14—pages 90–96

1. Arthur Carl Piepkorn, "Philipp Nicolai (1556-1608): Theologian, Mystic, Hymn Writer, Polemicist, and Missiologist: A Biobibliographical Survey," *Concordia Theological Monthly* 39:7 (July August 1968): 440.

2. Gerald S. Krispin, "A Mirror of Life in the Face of Death: A Study in the Pastoral Care of Philip Nicolai," *Logia* 7:2 (Eastertide 1998): 15.

3. Ibid., 38.

4. For images pertaining to this tradition, see Carolyn Diskant Muir, *Saintly Brides and Bridegrooms: The Mystic Marriage in Northern Renaissance Art* (London: Harvey Miller Publishers, 2012), 2–4.

5. Thanks for this correspondence from Paul Westermeyer, August 5, 2016.

6. Paul Westermeyer, *Hymnal Companion to Evangelical Lutheran Worship* (Minneapolis: Augsburg Fortress, 2010), 94.

7. "Wake, Awake," *Evangelical Lutheran Worship*, #436, and "Wake, O Wake," *One in Faith*, #353.

8. John Stacy Horn, "Singing Changes Your Brain," *Time,* August 16, 2013.

9. John Wesley, "Directions for Singing," *The United Methodist Hymnal* (Nashville: United Methodist Publishing House, 1989), vii.

10. For an example, see *Evangelical Lutheran Worship*, #268.

11. "Easter Proclamation," *Evangelical Lutheran Worship, Leaders Desk Edition* (Minneapolis: Augsburg Fortress, 2006), 647.

12. Most of these are in *Evangelical Lutheran Worship*, #439, #488, #244, #625, #638, #262.

13. W. G. Polack, *The Handbook to the Lutheran Hymnal* (St. Louis: Concordia Publishing House, 1942), 435.

Chapter 15—pages 97–104

1. "The Day of Resurrection" and "Come, You Faithful, Raise the Strain," *Evangelical Lutheran Worship*, #361 and #363.

2. Andrew Louth, *St. John Damascene: Tradition and Originality in Byzantine Theology* (Oxford: Oxford University Press, 2002), 194–94.

3. St. John of Damascus, *Three Treatises on the Divine Images*, trans. and ed. Andrew Louth (Crestwood, NY: St. Vladimir's Seminary Press, 2003).

4. Ibid. (Treatise I:11), 26.

5. Ibid. (Treatise III:17), 96.

6. An excellent discussion is provided in Jeana Visel, *Icons in the Western Church: Toward a More Sacramental Encounter* (Collegeville, MN: Liturgical Press, 2016), for example, 74–75.

7. St. John of Damascus, *Three Treatises* (Treatise I:11), 26.

8. Ibid. (Treatise II:20), 75.

9. Liisa Heikkilä-Palo, *Pyhittäjä Herman Alaskalaisen Kirkko* (Helsinki, Finland: Maahenki Oy, 2013).

10. St. John of Damascus, *Three Treatises* (Treatise I:12), 27.

11. Ibid. (Treatise I:13), 27.

12. Martin Luther, "The Third Sermon, on Easter Sunday," trans. Kurt K. Hendel, *Luther's Works* 57 (St. Louis: Concordia Publishing House, 2016), 128.

13. Thanks to Anne Dawtry and Christopher Irvine, *Art and Worship*, Alcuin Liturgy Guide 2 (London: SPCK 2002), 5–6, for correctly stating the attitude of many Lutherans on this issue.

14. See, for example, Hans Hartman and Kerstin Selén, *Väggarna Talar: Albertus Pictors Kyrkor* (Jarläså, Sweden: Ordbruket AB, 2009).

15. *Lojo Kykka* (Lojo Församling, Finland: Tavastehus, 1991).

16. St. John of Damascus, *Three Treatises* (Treatise I:18), 32.

17. Judith Herrin, *Women in Purple: Rulers of Medieval Byzantium* (Princeton, NJ: Princeton University Press, 2001).

18. See Victoria M. Young, *Saint John's Abbey Church: Marcel Breuer and the Creation of a Modern Sacred Space* (Minneapolis: University of Minnesota Press, 2014).

19. Roger Wedell, "Berdyaev and Rothko: Transformative Visions," *Art, Creativity, and the Sacred: An Anthology in Religion and Art*, ed. Diane Apostolos-Cappadona (New York: Crossroad, 1988), 308.

20. See John W. Cook, "Where the Spirit Abides," *Visual Theology: Forming and Transforming the Community through the Arts*, ed. Robin M. Jensen and Kimberly J. Vrudny (Collegeville, MN: Liturgical Press, 2009), 173, for "the church of the future" as interfaith sacred space.

21. Frank Whitford, *Bauhaus* (London: Thames and Hudson, 1984).

22. Richard S. Vosko, *God's House is Our House: Re-imagining the Environment for Worship* (Collegeville, MN: Liturgical Press, 2006), 5, 19.

23. See, for example, Bert Daelemans, *Spiritus Loci: A Theological Method for Contemporary Church Architecture* (Leiden, The Netherlands: Brill, 2015).

24. See Dawtry and Irvine, *Art and Worship*, 9.

25. John Cook, "A Willem de Kooning Triptych and St. Peter's Church," *Theological Education* 31:1 (1994), 70. In the interests of full disclosure:

Cook analyzes his sense of my role in this debate, 61–62. See also Maura Behrenfeld, "Liturgical Experiences through Abstract Art," *Studia Liturgica* 47:1 (2017), 113–18.

26. This despite the plea for non-figurative art in Frédéric Debuyst, *Modern Architecture and Christian Celebration* (Richmond, VA: John Knox Press, 1968), 76–77.

27. Olav Dag Hauge, et al., *Bildets Budskap: Takmaleriene i Oslo Domkirke* (Oslo, Norway: Snorre, 2008).

28. Sandra Bowden, et al. eds., *Beauty Given by Grace: The Biblical Prints of Sadao Watanabe* (Baltimore, MD: Square Halo Books, 2012), 104–107.

29. Margaret R. Miles, *Image as Insight: Visual Understanding in Western Christianity and Secular Culture* (Boston: Beacon Press, 1985), 148–49.

30. For example, www.lectionary.library.Vanderbilt.edu; Augsburg Fortress's www.sundaysandseasons.org; and David Stancliffe's e-books, *The Gospels in Art and Music* (London: SPCK, 2013, 2014, 2015).

31. Janet R. Walton, *Art and Worship: A Visual Connection* (Collegeville, MN: Liturgical Press, 1988), 19–30.

32. St. John of Damascus, *Three Treatises* (Treatise 11:14), 71.

Chapter 16—pages 105–11

1. See Job Kozhamthadam, "Reflection of the Trinitarian 'Structure' in the Material World," in *The Discovery of Kepler's Laws: The Interaction of Science, Philosophy, and Religion* (Notre Dame: University of Notre Dame, 1994), 29–34.

2. From William H. Donahue, trans., "New Astronomy," *The Faith of Scientists in Their Own Words*, ed. Nancy K. Frankenberry (Princeton, NJ: Princeton University Press, 2008), 47.

3. Ibid., 48–49.

4. Ibid., 47.

5. Frank C. Senn, *Christian Liturgy, Catholic and Evangelical* (Minneapolis: Fortress Press, 1997), 329–38.

6. Eugene TeSelle, "Creeds, Symbols, and Confessions of Faith," *The Cambridge Dictionary of Christianity*, ed. Daniel Patte (Cambridge, UK: Cambridge University Press, 2010), 285–87.

7. "The Athanasian Creed," *The Lutheran Hymnal* (St. Louis: Concordia Publishing House, 1941), 53.

8. Julian of Norwich, "A Revelation of Love," 51:273–75, *The Writings of Julian of Norwich*, 287.

9. For a sustained discussion, see my "Liturgical Considerations of the Myth of the Crown," *Worship* 66 (1992), 482–97.

10. A more accurate translation is "All Creatures, Worship God Most High," *Evangelical Lutheran Worship*, #835.

11. From Donahue, "New Astronomy," 53.

Chapter 17—pages 112–19

1. Dorothy Day, *The Long Loneliness* (New York: Harper and Row, 1952), 141.

2. *Catholic Worker*, January 1972, cited in Jim Forest, *All Is Grace: A Biography of Dorothy Day* (Maryknoll, NY: Orbis Books, 2011), 254.

3. Pope Francis's address to the joint meeting of Congress, September 24, 2015.

4. Day, *Long Loneliness*, 231.

5. Ibid., 270.

6. Patrick Jordan, *Dorothy Day: Love in Action* (Collegeville, MN: Liturgical Press, 2015), 40.

7. Catherine of Siena, *The Prayers*, 80.

8. The General Prayer, *Common Service Book of the Lutheran Church* (Philadelphia: The Board of Publication of the United Lutheran Church in America, 1917), 19–20.

9. Julie O'Connor, *The Moral Vision of Dorothy Day: A Feminist Perspective* (New York: Crossroad, 1991), 31.

10. See Day's chapter "Community" in *The Long Loneliness*, 222–35.

11. William D. Miller, *All Is Grace: The Spirituality of Dorothy Day* (Garden City, NY: Doubleday and Company, 1987), 3.

12. Cited in Jordan, *Dorothy Day*, 88.

13. From Robert Ellsberg, ed., "The Third Hour," in *By Little and By Little: The Selected Writings of Dorothy Day* (New York: Alfred Z. Knopf, 1983), 184.

Chapter 19—pages 123–29

1. Bonaventure, *The Life of St. Francis*, trans. Ewert Cousins (New York: Paulist Press, 1978), 225.

2. For example, see Augustine Thompson, *Francis of Assisi: A New Biography* (Ithaca, NY: Cornell University Press, 2012), the biography on pages 2–145, a discussion of the sources on pages 149–278; or André Vauchez, *Francis of Assisi: The Life and Afterlife of a Medieval Saint*, trans.

Michael F. Cusato (New Haven: Yale University Press, 2012), over half the volume on Francis's afterlife; or John Tolan, *Saint Francis and the Sultan: The Curious History of a Christian and Muslim Encounter* (New York: Oxford University Press, 2009), in which a detailed discussion of the sources precedes and informs the text.

3. See, for example, Jacques Dalarun, "The Great Secret of Francis," in *The Stigmata of Francis of Assisi: New Studies, New Perspectives* (St. Bonaventure, NY: The Franciscan Institute, 2006), 9–26.

4. See, for example, Chiara Frugoni, *Francis of Assisi* (New York: Continuum, 1998), 141, and Donald Spoto, *Reluctant Saint: The Life of Francis of Assisi* (New York: Viking, 2002), 194.

5. Marion A. Habig, ed., "Canticle of Brother Sun," *St. Francis of Assisi, Writings and Early Biographies: English Omnibus of the Sources of the Lord of St. Francis* (Chicago: Franciscan Herald Press, 1973), 130–31.

6. Colin Buchanan, *The Kiss of Peace* (Bramcote, England: Grove Books, 1982), 80.

7. Thomas Day, *Why Catholics Can't Sing: The Culture of Catholicism and the Triumph of Bad Taste* (New York: Crossroad, 1990), 6.

8. Cited in Spoto, *Reluctant Saint*, 176.

Chapter 20—pages 130–36

1. Brother Roger, *The Sources of Taizé* (Chicago: GIA Publications, 2000), 49.

2. Dirk G. Lange, "Recovering Communal Prayer: The Witness of the Community of Taizé," *Liturgy* 30, no. 4 (2015): 28.

3. Ibid., 32.

4. Brother Roger, *The Taizé Experience* (Collegeville, MN: Liturgical Press, 1990), 57.

5. Brother Roger, *Festival* (Taizé: Les Presses de Taizé, 1973), 53.

6. See the plea of Thomas E. Fitzgerald, *The Ecumenical Movement: An Introductory History* (Westport, CT: Phraeger, 2004), 222.

7. Hélène Cixous, *The Hélène Cixous Reader*, ed. Susan Sellers (New York: Routledge, 1994), xvii, 100.

8. Jason Brian Santos, *A Community Called Taizé* (Downers Grove, IL: IVP Books, 2008), 36–37.

9. See Judith Marie Kubicki, *Liturgical Music as Ritual Symbol: A Case Study of Jacques Berthier's Taizé Music* (Leuven: Peeters, 1999), 51–70.

10. *Praying Together*, PDF English Language Liturgical Consultation, 1988.

11. Brother Roger of Taizé, *Essential Writings*, ed. Marcello Fidanzio (Maryknoll, NY: Orbis Books, 2006), 75.

Chapter 21—pages 137–42

1. Diarmaid MacCulloch, *Thomas Cranmer: A Life* (New Haven: Yale University Press, 1996), 417.

2. Leslie Williams, *Emblem of Faith Untouched: A Short Life of Thomas Cranmer* (Grand Rapids, MI: Eerdmans, 2016), 59.

3. MacCulloch, *Thomas Cranmer*, 616.

4. See Jonathan Dean, ed., *God Truly Worshipped: Thomas Cranmer and His Writings* (Norwich, UK: Canterbury Press, 2012), 111.

5. Ibid., 112.

6. Ibid., 101.

7. Thanksgiving at the Table X, *Evangelical Lutheran Worship*, 69.

8. Per Harling, "You Are Holy," *Evangelical Lutheran Worship*, #525.

9. Dean, *God Truly Worshipped*, 53.

Chapter 22—pages 143–49

1. Fiona Maddocks, *Hildegard of Bingen: The Woman of Her Age* (New York: Doubleday, 2001), 82–83.

2. Barbara Newman, "Sibyl of the Rhine," in *Voice of the Living Light: Hildegard of Bingen and Her World*, ed. Barbara Newman (Berkeley: University of California Press, 1998), 1 and n. 4.

3. Maddocks, *Hildegard of Bingen*, 150–54.

4. Constant Mews, "Religious Thinker," in *Voice of the Living Light*, 211, n. 24.

5. Beverly Mayne Kienzle, trans. and ed., *Hildegard of Bingen: Homilies on the Gospels* (Collegeville, MN: Liturgical Press, 2011), 92, 120.

6. See, for example, Paul Galbreath, *Leading into the World* (Lanham, MD: Rowman & Littlefield, 2014).

7. "O Holy Spirit, Root of Life," *Evangelical Lutheran Worship*, #399.

8. Barbara Newman, trans. and ed., *Saint Hildegard of Bingen, Symphonia: A Critical Edition of the "Symphonia armonie celestium revelationum"* (Ithaca: Cornell University Press, 1988), 140–41.

9. Hildegard of Bingen, *Scivias*, book II, vision 6, paragraphs 24 and 26, trans. Mother Columba Hart and Jane Bishop (New York: Paulist Press, 1990), 252–53.

10. Ibid., 255.

11. See Gisela H. Kreglinger, *The Spirituality of Wine* (Grand Rapids, MI: Eerdmans, 2016), especially chapter 3, "Wine in the Lord's Supper: Christ Present in Wine," 65–82.

12. Newman, *Symphonia*, #28, 150–51.

Chapter 23—pages 150–56

1. See www.dohnavurfellowship.org.

2. Amy Wilson-Carmichael, *Things as They Are: Mission Work in Southern India* (London: Morgan and Scott, 1903).

3. Elisabeth Elliot, *A Chance to Die: The Life and Legacy of Amy Carmichael* (Grand Rapids, MI: Fleming H. Revell, 1987), 295.

4. Wilson-Carmichael, *Things as They Are*, 23.

5. Ibid., 283.

6. Elliot, *Chance to Die*, 333.

7. Ibid., 176.

8. For this list, I am grateful to the following: *A Great Cloud of Witnesses: A Calendar of Commemorations* (New York: Church Publishing House, 2016); Robert Ellsberg, *Blessed Among Us: Day by Day with Saintly Witnesses* (Collegeville, MN: Liturgical Press, 2016); and Gail Ramshaw, *More Days for Praise* (Minneapolis: Augsburg Fortress, 2016).

9. Sally Fitzgerald, ed., *The Habit of Being: The Letters of Flannery O'Connor* (New York: Vintage Books, 1979), 354.

10. Elliot, *Chance to Die*, 122.

11. Richard H. Schmidt, *God Seekers: Twenty Centuries of Christian Spiritualities* (Grand Rapids, MI: William B. Eerdmans, 2008), 268.

Chapter 24—pages 157–64

1. George E. Gingras, trans., *Egeria: Diary of a Pilgrimage*, Ancient Christian Writers 38 (New York: Newman Press, 1970), 53. A better edition of Egeria's diary is Anne McGowan and Paul F. Bradshaw's *The Pilgrimage of Egeria: A New Translation of the Itinerarium Egeriae with Introduction and Commentary* (Collegeville, MN: Liturgical Press, 2018).

2. Gingras, *Egeria*, 111.

3. Ibid., 114.

4. Ibid., 126.

5. See John Wilkinson, trans. and ed., "The Old Armenian Lectionary," *Egeria's Travels to the Holy Land*, rev. ed. (Jerusalem: Ariel Publishing House, 1981), 267–71.

6. For a full list and discussion, see *Worship Guidebook for Lent and the Three Days* (Minneapolis: Augsburg Fortress, 2009), 127.

7. John F. Baldovin, *The Urban Character of Christian Worship: The Origins, Development, and Meaning of Stational Liturgy*, Orientalia Christiana Analecta 228 (Rome: Oriental Institute, 1987), 102–104.

8. Gregory of Nyssa, cited in Wilkinson, *Egeria's Travels*, 22.

9. Gingras, *Egeria*, 89.

Afterword—pages 165–67

1. Brian A. Wren, "Great God, Your Love Has Called Us," *Evangelical Lutheran Worship*, #358.

2. Herbert Musurillo, intro. and trans., "The Martyrdom of St. Polycarp," *The Acts of the Christian Martyrs* (Oxford: Clarendon Press, 1972), 7.

3. Augustine, "The Three Whom Jesus Raised to Life," *The Sunday Sermons of the Great Fathers*, trans. and ed. M. F. Toal (Chicago: Henry Regnery, 1963), IV:115–20.